Every DROP Counts

Exploring Water Science with Young Children in a Changing Climate

Ann Gadzikowski, MEd

Foreword by Alexa Yeo, MS

Published by Gryphon House, Inc.

P. O. Box 10, Lewisville, NC 27023

800.638.0928; 877.638.7576 [fax]

Visit us on the web at www.gryphonhouse.com.

Library of Congress Control Number: 2025930294

Bulk Purchase

Gryphon House books are available for special premiums and sales promotions as well as for fund-raising use. Special editions or book excerpts can also be created to specifications. For details, call 800.638.0928.

Disclaimer

Gryphon House, Inc., cannot be held responsible for damage, mishap, or injury incurred during the use of or because of activities in this book. Appropriate and reasonable caution and adult supervision of children involved in activities and corresponding to the age and capability of each child involved are recommended at all times. Do not leave children unattended at any time. Observe safety and caution at all times.

Dedication

To the creative and caring teachers at Families Together Cooperative Nursery School, who model every day how to support and trust children to play, learn, and solve problems together.

Acknowledgments

I am very grateful for the opportunity to collaborate on this project with my daughter, water scientist Alexa Yeo. Our conversations about hydrology, environmental science, and climate change inspired me to begin incorporating water science into my work with children. As a scientist and researcher, she has been a wonderful resource and a wise sounding board for me as I've continued to explore how to engage young children in learning about water in ways that are developmentally appropriate, scientifically accurate, and respectful of the planet.

Much of the content of this book is based on activities and curricula I developed at two early childhood programs over the past several years. I piloted a water science curriculum at School for Little Children in Evanston, Illinois, and I piloted a "Climate Explorers" curriculum at Families Together Cooperative Nursery School in Chicago. Many thanks to the children, teachers, and families who participated in those pilots.

A special thank-you goes to my friend Mary Lindberg who served as a writing partner during the drafting of this manuscript. Her kind and wise support was instrumental in my progress.

And a final huge thank-you to Stephanie Roselli and the team at Gryphon House for supporting this project and making this book a dream come true.

Table of Contents

Foreword

One of my earliest memories of being fascinated with water was when I painted our house. As a child, I loved to take a paintbrush and a bucket of water and "paint" with water on the outside of the house. I brushed the water over the siding and watched as the color of the wood became darker for a short time before it slowly dried and went back to its original shade. It strikes me now how formative these water-play experiences can be to young children.

Fast forward to today, and I'm a researcher at Colorado School of Mines pursuing a doctorate in hydrology. My research focuses on waves and coastal hazards, hydrologic modeling, and precipitation. I hope my work will help improve forecasting and modeling of hydrologic conditions and allow people to recreate safely in coastal areas. But I didn't start out as a water scientist. I started as someone who wanted to build and design the world around us. I originally thought my civil engineering degree would lead me to designing and constructing bridges, buildings, and other infrastructure we interact with every day. But when I got into my degree, I discovered something I'd never heard of before: water resources engineering. The more I learned about it, the more I knew it was my path. Rather than working with the built environment, water resources engineering works with the natural environment and supports the infrastructure already in place. This is something that's not always protected, and yet it is arguably one of our most vital resources as humans. Water is essential for life on Earth. We use water to hydrate our bodies as well as for essential tasks such as bathing and cooking. We use water to grow crops that feed billions of people around the world. Without water, the world as we know it would not exist.

That's why teaching children about water at a young age is so important—not just to set children on a course to become water scientists or engineers, but for everyone to learn to be good stewards of our planet. The world is changing rapidly, and with it, our water resources, so it's our responsibility to set children up for success as best we can by teaching them the fundamentals that they can take into practice and work to preserve these resources. Not only is this about teaching fundamental lessons of water science, but it is also instilling the core belief that water is for everyone, and everyone deserves access to safe and clean water.

In this book, children will learn just that. What is water made of? Who is water for? Where does water come from? What will happen to our water? Those are just a few of the topics covered that will expose children to the fascinating world of water science. I believe that water will continue to become increasingly important in our everyday lives in ways most people will have never thought about today. A child growing up with water science knowledge in their back pocket will be one step ahead and equipped to succeed in a diverse set of careers while navigating a changing world. This book will also teach children the basics of the scientific process and the importance of curiosity and play in learning. For example, when testing out whether objects sink or float, children will develop a hypothesis, test it, and then come to a considered conclusion. The child's own play and curiosity will lead them to test out new ideas and work with others to solve problems.

One fundamental idea I hope children and teachers alike gain from this book is that the best course of action is for humans to learn to adapt our lives to water rather than forcing water to adapt to us—whether that means changing the way we manage and grow crops, where we build houses, or how we design our cities. Water is powerful. Both in excess and in dearth, water has the ability to shape communities, to affect people's health and wellness, and even to start wars.

We must instill in the next generation the idea that to live harmoniously with the water we so desperately need, we must respect water. My hope is that this book brings about an enthusiasm from children about water that will eventually grow to change the trajectory of our water resources. We need both creativity and knowledge to bring about meaningful change in a time when much is uncertain. I think any classroom that can add water to their curriculum is playing an integral part in setting up the next generation of water scientists and stewards. And something as simple as playing at the beach, or even painting a house with water, could be the first step in this journey.

Alexa Yeo

Water Scientist and Hydrology Researcher
Colorado School of Mines

Introduction

What's so transparent it's almost invisible, can shift its shape to fit into any path or container, has the power to dissolve many substances, and provides essential care to every living thing, from tiny ants to gigantic blue whales?

The answer, of course, is water. Water has all of these superpowers.

At the same time, water is so commonplace and ordinary, you might not even think about it. How many times have you used water today? Did you brew a pot of coffee? take a shower? rinse your breakfast dishes? Not to mention all the water pulsing through your own veins and hydrating every cell in your body. As we begin to think about water, let's consider why this resource matters so much in our daily lives and beyond.

Why Water Matters

Water has become one of the world's most valuable resources. For example, the water supply in the Colorado River Valley, called "ground zero for climate change in the United States" by The Nature Conservancy, has been significantly diminished in recent years, resulting in new restrictions on the use of water in homes and schools across several states (The Nature Conservancy, n.d.). The importance of keeping our water supply safe and clean is highlighted by events such as the Flint, Michigan, water crisis, which has resulted in drinking water contaminated by lead (Denchak,

2024). While the young children in our preschool and kindergarten classrooms may not be aware of these events and issues, they do know that water is an important part of our daily lives. Children drink water, bathe in water, and play with water every day. And they will be growing up in a world in which water supplies, water safety, and water infrastructures are significantly affected by climate change. The good news is that children can learn more about these issues and can begin to think about them in meaningful and hopeful ways.

Empowering Children as Problem-Solvers and Change Makers

We need not frighten children with predictions of future catastrophe. The most important role of the child is to be a child. We must protect children's right to play and to experience joy. There is an important and urgent role for young children in combating climate change, but it is a hopeful one. The role of the child includes experiencing the natural world as a place of beauty and wonder. It is our responsibility, as parents, teachers, and caregivers, to nurture and support children's relationships with the natural world. In the stressful environments of a changing climate, we can no longer assume that all children will have the opportunity to play outside and appreciate the beauty and wonder of plants, animals, and landscapes. We must actively provide these opportunities. Children construct a relationship with nature through their senses—what they see, hear, smell, touch, and perhaps even taste, such as the light filtered by the leaves of a tree, the song of a bird, the scent of lilacs, or the rough grains of sand under bare feet. Even children in harsh urban environments or stark settings such as refugee camps—especially children in these settings—benefit from safe, open-ended, active exploration in an outdoor natural space.

Importantly, the role of the child includes engaging in creative, social, and exploratory play. Through play, children become scientists, engineers, and innovators. Through play children learn to observe, wonder, and understand. Play empowers children as change agents because it prepares them for imagining and constructing solutions to problems. This is especially true of construction play and pretend play.

As stated in the white paper published by LEGO, *Where Global Science Meets Playful Learning: Implications for Home, School, Cities, and Digital Spaces* (Hirsh-Pasek et al., 2022):

> New knowledge requires exploration, trial and error, testing of a vision, development of a design, and finally, the drive to take that spark into the marketplace of ideas. How do we create an environment that nurtures the drive for exploration and discoveries?

It is not difficult to imagine that the young child today who is playing on a beach, digging canals in the sand, and building bridges out of sticks will one day be an engineer who constructs a seawall to protect a coastline community. With this in mind, families and educators must provide opportunities for children to play with both natural materials as well as manufactured toys, in both indoor and outdoor settings.

About This Book

This book is organized into eleven chapters. While each chapter builds on the ideas and content in the previous chapters, each stands alone as a complete guide for teachers on a specific water-related topic.

Chapter 1: Who Needs Water?

Learning about water is meaningful to young children because they use and observe water every day. Activities focus on the practical uses of water, such as cooking and bathing, as well as the presence of water in the natural world.

Chapter 2: What Is Water?

This chapter presents the scientific characteristics and properties of water (such as states of matter) through play and developmentally appropriate activities and experiments, such as using measuring cups, flashlights, and magnifying glasses to discover that water is a liquid and, if it is clean, it can appear colorless.

Chapter 3: Water and Weather

Using children's direct sensory experiences, as well as playful activities and picture books, the content of this chapter teaches about rain, snow, storms, and other weather phenomena.

Chapter 4: Hot, Cold, and In Between

This chapter addresses concepts related to observing and measuring the temperature of water and builds on concepts related to states of matter (ice, liquid, gas) introduced in chapter 2. Also included in this chapter is guidance on teaching children how to use authentic scientific tools, such as thermometers.

Chapter 5: Water and Plants

All plants need water to grow. In this chapter, we explore how plants receive water from natural sources such as rain, as well as human sources such as irrigation systems.

Chapter 6: Fish and Other Life in and around Water

Dramatic play, picture books, and creative art projects engage children in learning about the fish and other sea creatures who live in and around the water, in ponds and streams as well as in large bodies of water such as the ocean.

Chapter 7: Boats and Other Things that Float

The content of this chapter goes beyond the classic "Sink or Float?" sorting activities and dives deep into the question of why. Activities and resources provide guidance on developmentally appropriate ways to teach about density and buoyancy.

Chapter 8: Water and the Built Environment

The built environment includes structures such as bridges, canals, and dams that are constructed in relation to water. Construction play and projects using blocks, sand, and bricks are at the center of this chapter.

Chapter 9: Pipes and Plumbing

This chapter focuses on one specific category of the built environment—the infrastructure involved in moving clean water into our homes and buildings as well as the safe removal of dirty water.

Chapter 10: Where Does Water Come From?

Building on the water processing concepts introduced in the previous chapter, the content of this chapter provides guidance for introducing children to the water cycle, nature's own recycling program, as well as the water processing systems that keep our water clean.

Chapter 11: Caring for Water and Our Planet

The book concludes with a chapter devoted to developmentally appropriate environmental science and conservation. Activities and resources emphasize the role of communities in working together to protect our planet and our most valuable resource—water.

Each chapter begins with an explanation of why this topic is important and appropriate for young children. Every chapter includes the following sections:

- **Learning Objectives:** A summary of relevant learning objectives and how they align with Head Start Early Learning Outcomes Framework, Next Generation Science Standards (NGSS), and the National Association for the Education of Young Children (NAEYC) Early Learning Program Accreditation Standards and Assessment Items. Note: The learning objectives reference the 2022 edition of NAEYC standards rather than the more recent 2025 accreditation update. This is because the 2022 version includes recommended practices, experiences, and materials that are specifically relevant to water science explorations. Overall, the ideas presented in this book are well aligned with both the 2022 and the 2025 editions of NAEYC standards.
- **Background Information for Educators:** Explanations of scientific concepts that teachers need to know to feel comfortable teaching this content
- **Explore:** Ideas for introducing the chapter topic through exploratory experiences and provocations
- **Play:** Open-ended play activities that introduce, support, and deepen concepts and understanding
- **Experiment:** Teacher-facilitated activities and science experiments that demonstrate key science concepts

The chapters also include special features, such as Vocabulary, Ask a Water Scientist, and Recommended Children's Books.

- The **Vocabulary** feature provides key terms and definitions related to the chapter topic. This information supports the development of your own content knowledge about unfamiliar science concepts and the definitions serve as a resource to help you explain concepts to children in the classroom.
- The **Ask a Water Scientist** feature provides answers to common questions from both teachers and children that might arise during activities. The answers are written by water scientist Alexa Yeo, who serves as the content expert for this book.
- The **Recommended Children's Books** feature offers a few titles of quality picture books that present water science concepts in ways that are both accurate and developmentally appropriate. These lists are not comprehensive but include handpicked titles that are especially engaging and fun.

Learning Objectives

Whether we are following a predesigned curriculum sequence or creating curriculum based on children's emerging interests, we can look to several key resources to help us create learning objectives related to water science for preschool and kindergarten. Some of those resources include the Head Start Early Learning Outcomes Framework, NGSS, and the NAEYC Early Learning Program Accreditation Standards and Assessment Items.

Head Start Early Learning Outcomes Framework includes three goals relevant to the broad topic of water science: Domain: Scientific Reasoning, Sub-Domain: Scientific Inquiry, and Goals under the Scientific Inquiry sub-domain:

- **Goal P-SCI 1.** Child observes and describes observable phenomena (objects, materials, organisms, and events).
- **Goal P-SCI 2.** Child engages in scientific talk.
- **Goal P-SCI 3.** Child compares and categorizes observable phenomena (U.S. Department of Health and Human Services, Administration for Children and Families, Office of Head Start, 2015).

These goals are relevant to any preschool classroom, whether part of the federal Head Start program or not. These guidelines remind us that young children are natural scientists and child-directed play is an effective method for practicing scientific reasoning and scientific inquiry.

Next Generation Science Standards (NGSS) name important science and engineering practices that are relevant to explorations of water, including:

- Asking questions and defining problems
- Planning and carrying out investigations
- Analyzing and interpreting data
- Constructing explanations
- Obtaining, evaluating, and communicating information (National Research Council, 2013)

NAEYC accreditation standards are quality benchmarks for programs rather than learning objectives for children. Topic 2.G Science addresses program plans for experiences and materials that support children's scientific inquiry and knowledge through observation, the use of simple tools, representation of findings, and the use of scientific terminology and vocabulary (NAEYC, 2022).

Throughout the NAEYC accreditation standards, science learning is described as rooted in children's sensory experiences—discovery, exploration, and curiosity related to what children see, touch, hear, taste, and smell. Many of the science topics and activities named in the accreditation guidelines are related to water, including weather, the structure and properties of matter (such as floating and sinking), and the behavior of materials (such as dissolving and melting). Teachers are encouraged to discuss scientific concepts in the context of everyday conversations, using relevant scientific terminology such as *melt*, *freeze*, *hot*, *cold*, *earth*, *weather*, and *life*.

Each chapter of this book is built around learning objectives that are informed by these three resources as well as current research in the field of child development. The objectives are worded and structured in ways that help you scaffold children's learning experiences, provide meaningful, play-based contexts for learning, and create foundations for future learning.

Let's Dive In!

It's hard to imagine a topic more universally relevant and meaningful than water. The ideas presented in this book will empower both teachers and children to dive into the study and exploration of water with curiosity and creativity. I invite you to swim through this book like a fish in fresh water, taking what you need and always moving forward.

Chapter One:

Who Needs Water?

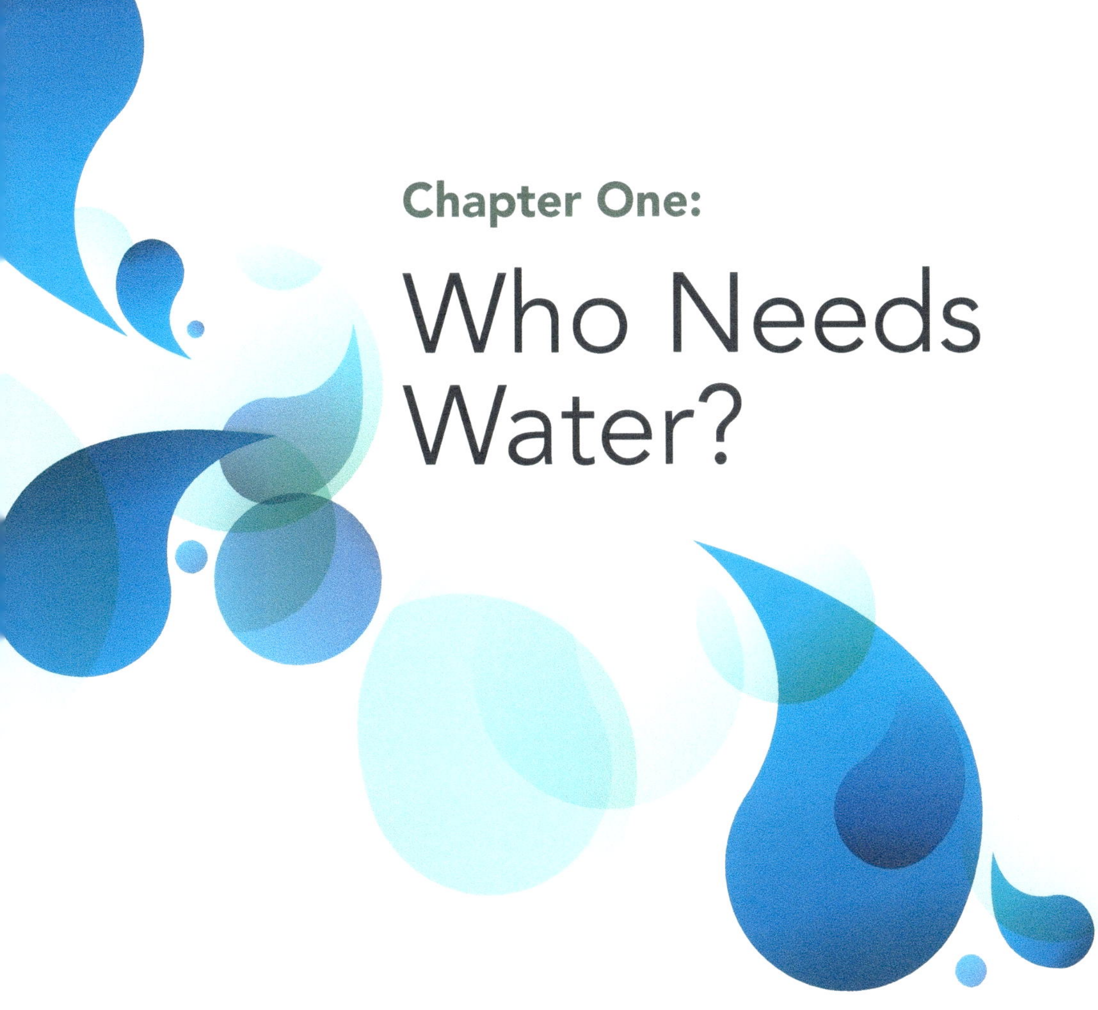

Two preschool children, Bela and James, are playing with water in the classroom sensory table. Bela scoops water into a cup, nearly filling it. James holds an empty bowl in both hands and says to Bela, "I need some too." Bela pours the water from her cup into James's bowl.

Bela and James look at the water in the bowl, which is now about half full.

James says, "More!" Bela scoops more water into the cup and pours it into James's bowl, now filling it. In fact, some of the water splashes onto James's hands and arms. He shrieks with surprised pleasure when the water touches his skin, and both children laugh.

"More!" says James. Bela fills the cup again and pours the water into the now-full bowl. Water runs over the sides of the bowl and, again, some splashes onto James's hands and arms.

"More!" says James again. Bela smiles and continues pouring water into the full bowl.

Every child is already a water expert. Every child knows the feeling of water on their skin.

Like Bela and James in the scenario above, children often experience a sense of joyous curiosity when they engage with water. In early childhood classrooms, when water is offered as a play choice, most children will eagerly choose to play with it. As Bela and James demonstrated, water is a source of fun and provides opportunities for social connections between children.

Water play can also soothe children. Experienced educators and caregivers know that a stressed or agitated child will likely be calmed by playing with water. Children know that water is a source of comfort and care. Children ask for a drink of water when they are thirsty. They enjoy the relief of a cool drink of water on a hot day.

Children drink water, they bathe in it, and they play with it. They see their families cook with water and use it to water their gardens and plants. They see water in the form of rain coming down from the sky. Children splash in the puddles formed by the rain. Water is everywhere in the lives of young children.

Children are eager to learn about topics and ideas that are relevant and meaningful to their direct experiences in the world. Learning about water is meaningful to young children because they use and observe it every day. In this chapter, we'll focus on play experiences and curriculum activities that demonstrate and explore the practical uses of water, such as drinking, cooking, and bathing, as well as the presence of water in the natural world.

Learning Objectives

As discussed in the introduction of this book, the Head Start Early Learning Outcomes Framework affirms the importance of exploring water science in preschool. Additionally, the Head Start framework specifically refers to the practical uses of water in children's daily lives.

For example, the Head Start learning goal for infants and toddlers related to causal relationships refers to children's first independent experiences using a water faucet and carrying a cup of water. Similarly, a learning goal for preschoolers (by thirty-six months) expands on children's daily experiences with water at home and at school with a focus on cause and effect.

> **Sub-Domain:** Exploration and Discovery
>
> **Goal IT-C 2.** Child uses understanding of causal relationships to act on social and physical environments.
>
> **Developmental Progression 16–36 Months**
> Identifies the cause of an observed outcome, such as the tower fell over because it was built too high. Predicts outcomes of actions or events, such as turning the faucet will make water come out.
>
> **Indicators (by 36 Months)**
> Anticipates some cause and effects of own actions, such as what happens while running with a cup of water (U.S. Department of Health and Human Services, Administration for Children and Families, Office of Head Start, 2015).
>
> Building on these early learning experiences of infants and toddlers and progressing through preschool, the important role of water in children's daily lives is also reflected in the Head Start goal related to hygiene and self-care.

Sub-Domain: Healthy, Safety, and Nutrition

Goal P-PMP 4. Child demonstrates personal hygiene and self-care skills.

Indicators (by 60 Months)
Washes hands with soap and water. Knows to do this before eating, after using the bathroom, or after blowing nose (U.S. Department of Health and Human Services, Administration for Children and Families, Office of Head Start, 2015).

Based on the Head Start Early Learning Outcomes Framework, as well as NAEYC accreditation standards and NGSS practices, the following learning objectives are developmentally responsive and directly related to the practical uses of water in children's daily lives. The four objectives are worded and structured in ways that help you scaffold children's learning experiences, provide meaningful, play-based contexts for learning, and create foundations for future learning.

Chapter 1 Learning Objectives

1. Support children's growing understanding of the importance of water in their daily lives for practical purposes such as bathing, cleaning, and eating.
2. Increase children's awareness of water in their environment and their ability to observe water science phenomena.
3. Inspire curiosity about water and document children's questions and wonderings about water science.
4. Provide opportunities for regular water play indoors and outdoors.

Background Information for Educators

What do you need to know to support children's growing awareness and understanding of water? Look around your classroom and notice where water is present or where there are sources of water.

- Do you have a sink with a faucet or other sources of running water?
- Do you have a drinking fountain or access to a water pitcher for drinking water?
- Do teachers or children keep individual water bottles in the classroom?
- Do you have a sensory table or bin that can be filled with water? (Is it positioned near a sink or faucet?)
- In the art area, do you have water available to mix with paint or rinse brushes?
- What about containers of water that are used for other purposes, such as a watering can for plants?
- Do you have any sensory toys that are filled with water, such as sensory viewers or squeeze toys?

- Do you have a fish tank or aquarium that is filled with water?
- Do you have a classroom pet who drinks from a water dish?
- Do you have plants in wet soil or flowers in vases?
- Do you have windows to the outdoors where rain, ice, or condensation might form?
- Do you notice any condensation on or near air conditioners, heaters, or vents?

Observing and noticing all the locations and sources of water is a *water inventory*. Conducting a water inventory will help you think about (or rethink) the ways you will expand or add water play, provide for water experiences, and guide water conversations in your classroom. An increased awareness of where, how, and when water is used in your environment will also help you make connections between the children's daily experiences with water and water science.

Practical Life Skills

How many times a day do children in your classroom wash their hands? In some full-day settings, children might wash their hands more than a dozen times a day. How many times a day do children flush a toilet? How many times do they drink water from a cup or a drinking fountain? Each of these interactions with water is a learning experience. Children are learning to care for themselves, and they are also learning about water. As you'll see in the chapters of this book, we can use each experience with water as an opportunity to observe, wonder, discuss, and explore the unique characteristics of water.

Explore

Open-ended play activities provide opportunities to introduce, support, and deepen children's understanding about water. As teachers, our role is to set the stage for child-directed play and trust that children will discover exciting ideas related to water and pose meaningful questions about water. In preschool classrooms, the easiest way to encourage children to explore water inside is by inviting them to play with it in a sensory table.

Indoor Water Play with a Sensory Table

In the early childhood program where I work, each classroom is equipped with a large sensory table, which is a rectangular bin on legs. A hole in the bottom of the bin allows for draining the water and a plug for the hole keeps the water in. Sometimes, the sensory table is filled with loose materials like sand, but most of the time we fill it with water. By "fill" I mean just a few inches deep. We keep a bucket under the drain in case a child pulls the plug. And we like to add a flat wooden plank across the middle so children have a place to set things down while they play.

While a commercial sensory table is ideal for water play, a large, flat bin will also work for water play. Make sure the table or bin is clean before filling it. You can fully sanitize the surface by spraying it with a diluted bleach solution (no more than 1 teaspoon of bleach per 1 cup of water). Allow the sanitizing solution to air dry or wipe clean before filling the container with water for play.

Water play containers need not be filled very high with water—just a few inches of water is plenty (more than that might cause splashing or spills, and too much water makes it hard to empty and clean the play container afterward).

Health and Safety Considerations

Water play requires attention to a few particular health and safety concerns. Check your local health and safety regulations for guidance. NAEYC (2022) accreditation standards include guidance regarding water play, such as not allowing children to drink the water and not allowing children with sores on their hands to play in a water container used by other children. Water should be clean and completely drained and replaced between groups of children or should continuously flow into the container and out through a drain.

In addition to potential hazards related to germs, water play also presents the risk of accidental drowning. Infants and toddlers should never be allowed to play with buckets of water. Preschool and school-age children should always be supervised by sight and sound in all areas with access to water, including containers filled with just a few inches of water.

What other items might be needed for water play? Consider what might happen if children were invited to play with only water and nothing else. Children would likely use their hands to touch and explore the water. They might try to make something happen by pushing or patting the water. What might happen next? Splashing!

There's nothing wrong with splashing around in water, especially when water play takes place outside on a warm day. But for water play indoors, you'll probably want to provide children with some toys or tools that will allow children to explore, pretend, and play without causing a tidal wave.

Simple containers such as **small cups and bowls** are essential for water play in a sensory table or bin. I especially like using clear or semi-clear containers so the children can see the water inside the container. **Measuring cups and measuring spoons** are wonderful water toys because they provide a range of sizes, they nest together, and they might inspire children to pretend they are cooking or baking. **Small muffin tins and little baking dishes** also inspire pretend play.

Spoons and ladles are also essential water play items. Providing a range of shapes and sizes adds variety to children's play, but keep in mind that you'll want multiples of popular items.

Sieves, colanders, and slotted spoons allow children to observe how water moves through a container. **Small pitchers with spouts** are fun for pouring—another way to move water from one container to another. A toy **tea set** with a small teapot is also fun to pour.

Items used for science experiments for older children can be repurposed for water play in a preschool classroom. **Test tubes, beakers, funnels, tubes, and eye droppers** are just a few examples.

Talking about Water

The most exciting and interesting conversations about water happen while children are playing with water and focus on the children's sensory experiences.

We can ask:

- "What does water look like?"
- "What does water feel like?"
- "What does water sound like?"
- "What does water smell like?"
- "What does water taste like?"

Play

Cups and spoons, sieves and pitchers, bowls and funnels—what a fun variety of items to play with! But how do teachers decide which materials to offer? We could rotate the materials, trying different combinations each time we set up the sensory bin or water table. Better yet, we could make intentional choices based on children's interests, needs, and abilities.

Sensory Play

When choosing which materials to offer children for water play, think about the child's sensory experience. Sight and touch are the senses that are most likely to be engaged during water play. Think about the color, shape, weight, and texture of the items children will use to pour or drip or measure the water. Consider also the temperature of water itself. The water you add to a sensory table at the beginning of the play session will eventually become "room temperature" but consider adding some warmer or cooler water during play. For example, suppose some children are using spoons and cups to pour and stir the water, and you notice that they are pretending to make ice cream. Adding some cold tap water to the sensory table could add some new interest and excitement to the pretend scenario and spark some new conversations and observations from the children.

Similarly, you could add a bit of food coloring or liquid water colors to the water in a sensory bin and observe how the color influences children's play. The color could be added in advance as you prepare the water for water play, or the children could watch you add the color to the water and observe how the color drops move through the water and become diluted.

Mild dish soap is another fun addition to water play. Just a few drops allow bubbles to form when the children stir and pour the water. Other fun additives include mint extracts or citrus essential oils that add pleasant aromas to the water. Be sure to check to see if children have any allergies or sensitivities before introducing these kinds of substances.

Danger: Glitter

In some preschool classrooms, water play is enhanced by the addition of a little decorative glitter to the water. However, recent research about the prevalence of microplastics in our water has called into question the use of glitter in homes and schools (Mahroof, 2023). Most glitter is made of plastic, which does not degrade. When glittery water is discarded and poured down our drains, small amounts of plastic can end up in our oceans and other bodies of water. These microplastics can be harmful to wildlife and to human health. Some craft companies make biodegradable glitter, but it can be costly.

Pretend Play

During water play, preschool children often take on roles and create pretend scenarios, such as the group of children who used the water to pretend to make ice cream. Kitchen items such as muffin tins, ice cream scoops, measuring spoons, and ladles inspire pretend cooking and baking.

Offering soap, sponges, and scrub brushes for water play can inspire pretend scenarios related to cleaning and bathing. Add some plastic dolls or toy animals and children are usually eager to give them a nice bath.

A water-filled sensory bin can also become a pretend ocean habitat with the addition of toy fish and other sea creatures. Natural materials such as shells and rocks also make wonderful additions to water play and can inspire creative pretend scenarios.

Water Play Outdoors

When children play with water outdoors, many of the same health and safety practices apply. Children should be well supervised in all areas with access to water, especially where there are containers filled with water. When outdoor water play involves running water, such as water from hoses or sprinklers, make sure that the water can drain away and does not create slippery surfaces.

A wonderfully messy and sensory play experience happens when water is added to sand or mud. Water can be added to dry sand in a sandbox. A patch of dirt can become a mud kitchen. A less-messy option for outdoor play is painting with water. Give each child a paintbrush and a cup of water and invite them to "paint" on a dry surface that will darken when wet, such as a concrete sidewalk or a stone wall.

Recommended Children's Books

***Hey, Water!* by Antoinette Portis**

This book provides a colorful introduction to the uses and characteristics of water. It works well as a read-aloud because the simple illustrations are easy to see and the brief text is easy to read.

***A Cool Drink of Water* by Barbara Kerley**

Kerley's book features photographs of people all over the world gathering water for drinking—from streams, wells, fountains, pumps, and more. These fascinating images from National Geographic demonstrate that not everyone has access to clean water from the tap.

Experiment

Activity: Water Hunt Indoors

Early in the chapter we discussed how teachers can take an inventory of all the examples and sources of water in their classroom. This type of activity can be adapted as a teacher-facilitated activity that helps children become more aware of the uses and characteristics of water in the world around them.

Prepare

Materials: clipboard and paper for each child, pencils or crayons, camera

Make a plan for how your class will document their discoveries during the water hunt. Some options include the following:

- Give each child or pair of children a clipboard with at least one page of paper and a pencil or crayon and invite them to draw a picture of what they find.
- Use a large whiteboard or chalkboard to list the class's discoveries.
- Take photos or video of the children's process.
- Give children sticky notes to attach to each place where they find water.

At group time, announce to the children, "We're going on a water hunt!" Explain that the water hunt is a time when everyone is the classroom is going to look around for examples of water. Briefly review with the children, "What is water?" and "What does water look like?"

Observe

Invite the children to walk around the classroom and look for examples of water. The most obvious examples might be a sensory table, a sink, and a fish tank. Children might also find pictures of water in books or objects, such as cups or bottles, that could contain water. Affirm all these suggestions as positive examples. As children hunt, ask questions that extend their thinking, such as, "Where might you find water for washing? for playing? for drinking?"

If possible, expand your search to nearby rooms, such as the school bathroom or kitchen.

Document

Create a list or some other form of documentation to record children's findings.

Reflect

Review the documentation as a large group or in smaller groups. Discussion prompts might include questions such as:

"What did you notice about the water in our classroom?

"How did you decide where to look?"

For each example, ask, "Where does this water come from? How did it get to our classroom?"

Listen to and record children's ideas. Also ask, "What questions do you have about water?"

Make note of these questions. You can use them to guide further explorations.

Encourage children and families to conduct a water hunt at home and compare the results. Talk about what is the same and what is different.

Activity: Water Walk Outdoors

Similar to the water hunt, take the children on a water walk outdoors.

Prepare

If possible, plan a walking route that will expose children to both natural and human-made sources of water. Examples of natural sources of water might include bodies of water such as creeks or streams, or evidence of rain such as puddles. Human-made sources of water might include a fountain or a sprinkler system.

Observe

As children discover examples of water outdoors, ask questions that will prompt them to observe details and consider the water sources, such as, "What do you see?" "What do you notice?" and "I wonder where that water comes from...." Guide the conversation to help children identify details that demonstrate the differences between natural sources of water and sources that are built by people. For example, children may notice that an outdoor faucet is attached to a pipe that is connected to a building. Or they may comment that puddles of water come from rain.

Document

Document children's discoveries and questions using the methods suggested in the water hunt activity above. Photographs work well for outdoor explorations. You can print or project some of the images for later review.

Reflect

Review the documentation and/or photos as a large group or in smaller groups. Prompt children to describe what they discovered with questions such as, "What did we see on our water walk?" "Where did we find the most water?" For each example, ask, "Where does this water come from?" Listen to and record children's ideas. Be sure to ask, "What questions do you have about water?" and take note of these questions.

To extend children's thinking, compare the indoor water hunt to the outdoor water walk. Talk about what is the same and what is different.

Think Ahead

The key takeaway from this chapter is that water is already an essential part of children's daily lives and most young children have a lot of prior knowledge about water. Daily water play, indoors and out, enhances children's joy in their sensory experiences with water and sparks their curiosity about water. Your own experiences and observations as a teacher will inform where you go next in your curriculum planning and in your conversations with children. In the following chapters, we build on these core experiences, expand children's curiosity about the science of water, and extend their content knowledge about how we live and grow on this amazing planet Earth.

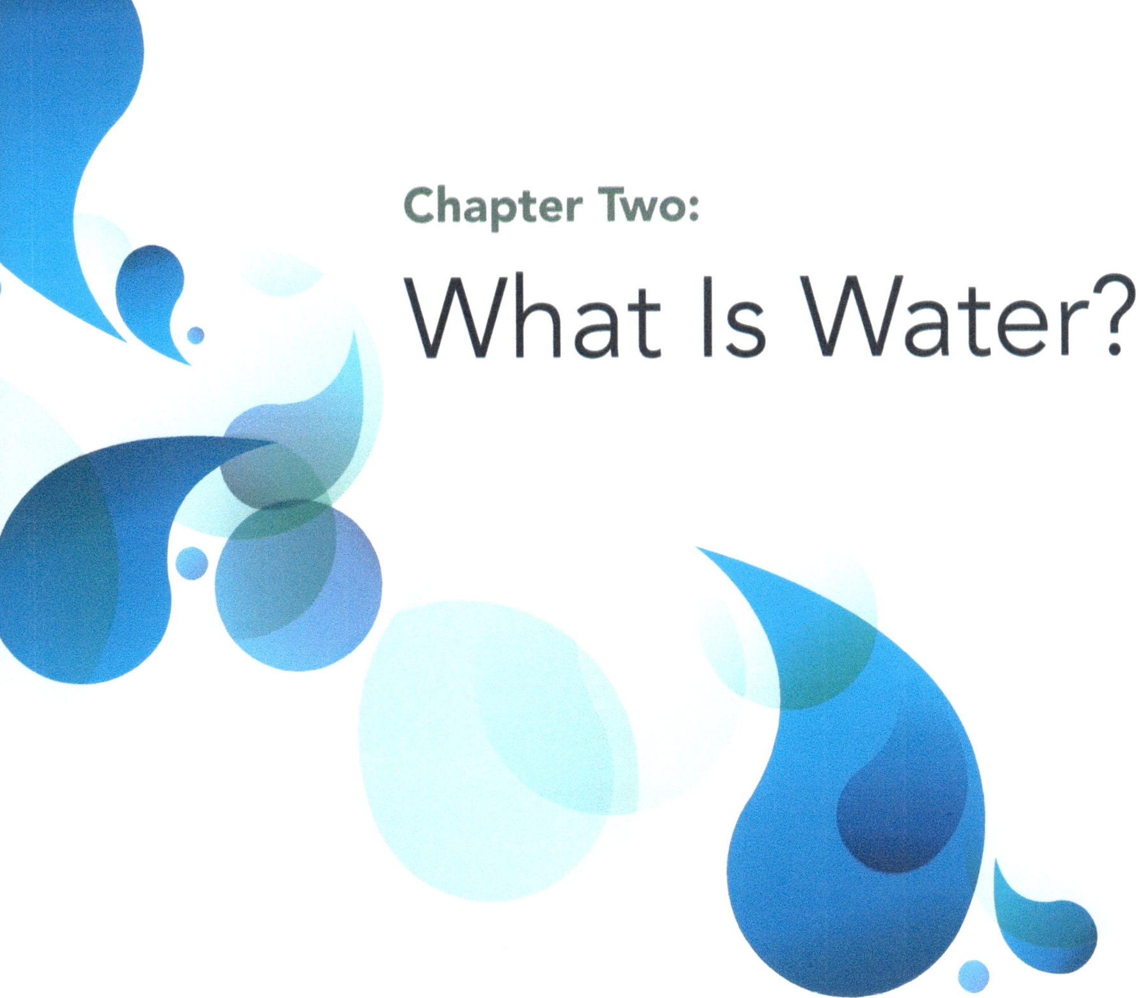

Chapter Two:

What Is Water?

Ms. Jasmine's preschool class is playing outdoors on the playground. Earlier, she filled several buckets with water to add to the sand in the sandbox. Now Ms. Jasmine is pouring the water from the buckets into the sand. Most of the children are gathered around the sandbox, excitedly cheering as the water soaks into the dry sand. The children laugh and clap when the water from each bucket splashes into the sandbox. One child exclaims, "The water disappears!" and another answers, "It's in the sand. It's dark now."

Meanwhile, the attention of one child is elsewhere. Olivia, age three, squats next to the last remaining bucket and plunges her hands into the water, wetting the sleeves of her shirt.

Ms. Jasmine watches Olivia carefully. The teacher's first thought is to tell Olivia to move away from the bucket. But, seeing that Olivia is safely positioned and the bucket will not spill, Ms. Jasmine decides to pause and observe for a moment.

Olivia keeps both of her hands in the bucket, her fingers submerged just below the surface of the water. Several minutes go by and Olivia remains in place, her concentration focused on the inside of the bucket. Olivia's head is low, her face close to the rim of the bucket.

Ms. Jasmine moves closer to Olivia and begins a conversation. "I noticed you put your hands in the water, Olivia."

Olivia is quiet for a moment and then whispers, "See my fingers."

Ms. Jasmine nods and peeks inside the bucket. "Yes, I can see your fingers in the water too."

Olivia slowly wiggles her fingers in the water.

Ms. Jasmine asks, "How does it feel?"

Olivia smiles as she wiggles her fingers. "Wet!"

Ms. Jasmine nods again. "Your hands are in the water. Your fingers are wet."

Olivia pulls her hands out of the water and holds them in the air. "Wet!" she yells.

Ms. Jasmine smiles. "Wet! Your hands are wet!"

Then Olivia helps Ms. Jasmine pour the final bucket of water into the sandbox.

Water's Characteristics

Water fascinates children in so many ways, it's hard to know, at any given moment, which characteristic of water—its movement, shape, or color—has captured a child's interest. In the vignette above, the main event for the class is the addition of water to the sandbox. The teacher has prepared buckets of water to add to the sandbox. She knows that the addition of water will change the consistency of the sand in the sandbox and has waited to pour the water until the children are outside with her so the children can observe how the water is absorbed by the dry sand.

And yet, in this scenario, there is one child who is not paying attention. Little Olivia is entirely focused on one lone bucket of water. She has plunged her hands into the water and then, surprisingly, stays in the same position for several minutes, her attention fixed on her own hands submerged in the water.

The teacher, Ms. Jasmine, could have insisted Olivia move away from the bucket. After all, the water in the buckets is clearly intended for another purpose. But Ms. Jasmine is as curious about Olivia's behavior as Olivia is curious about the water in the bucket. Ms. Jasmine waits and watches. She gives Olivia a little time and space to explore the water with her senses—primarily sight and touch. Perhaps Olivia is noticing the transparent quality of water. Perhaps she's noticing the cooling sensation of the water on her skin.

This scenario demonstrates that sometimes the experience the teacher plans and prepares (adding water to the sandbox) can have an additional or different meaning for a particular child. Just slowing down for a moment or two can open the door to new explorations and discovery.

Learning Objectives

While NAEYC's (2022) accreditation standards are quality benchmarks for programs rather than learning objectives for children, it may be helpful to note that the behavior of materials such as liquids and solids is specifically mentioned under Topic 2.G Science as key content.

The following learning objectives are informed by resources such as Head Start, NGSS, and NAEYC as well as current research in the field of child development and science education. The four objectives are worded and structured in ways that help you scaffold children's learning experiences, provide meaningful, play-based contexts for learning, and create foundations for future learning.

Chapter 2 Learning Objectives

1. Support children's growing understanding of water as a liquid.
2. Provide opportunities for children to practice observing and discussing characteristics of water: the movement, the shape, and the color.
3. During regular water play indoors and outdoors, expose children to concepts and vocabulary related to the characteristics of water.
4. Conduct teacher-facilitated science activities and experiments that demonstrate the characteristics of water such as the movement of liquid water and the translucent quality of clean water.

Background Information for Educators

If a child asks, "What is water?" how do you answer?

You might start by describing things you can do with water. "Water is something you drink." You might talk about where water comes from (rain, rivers, pipes) or talk about how we use water (for cooking, drinking, or cleaning). You might say, "Water is a liquid." But then the child might ask, "What's a liquid?"

What Is a Liquid?

The term *liquid* usually doesn't appear in school curriculum until the primary grades, when students learn the three states of matter: solid, liquid, and gas. Yet, many preschool children have probably heard the word liquid and it's appropriate for preschool teachers to use the word in context, providing examples of liquids and the things a liquid can do.

For example:

A liquid is something you drink.

A liquid is wet.

Water is a liquid. Milk is a liquid. Juice is a liquid.

Rain is a liquid.

A liquid is something that can spill.

A liquid can be poured.

Vocabulary

Water: a clear liquid that, when pure, can have no color, taste, or smell; that falls from clouds as rain; that forms puddles, streams, lakes, and seas; and that is used for drinking, washing, and more

Liquid: a substance that can flow freely

The Movement of Water

As teachers who talk to children about water, it may be helpful to review our own content knowledge a bit to include some additional facts about liquid water. If you ask a scientist, "What is water?" they might say that water is a substance composed of the chemical elements of hydrogen and oxygen. You've probably heard water referred to as "H2O." That's because a water molecule is made up of two hydrogen (H) atoms and one oxygen (O) atom. Molecules are very, very small, and atoms are even smaller, so small we can't even see them. A single drop of water contains billions of water molecules.

Knowing that water is made up of tiny molecules helps us better understand the nature of liquids and how they move. Young children are often fascinated by the movement of liquid water. Still water responds to our touch by splashing, flowing, and sloshing. We can pour water from one container to another. When water spills, it moves across the surface it touches.

Several of the activities in this chapter challenge children to consider the question "What is the shape of water?" We can observe that each time water moves into a space, it forms the shape of the container that holds it.

Ask a Water Scientist

Why does water take on the shape of whatever container it's in?

Water molecules move freely. Liquid water takes the shape of its container because the forces that hold the molecules together in a liquid are weaker than those in a solid, allowing the molecules to flow and slip past one another (National Aeronautics and Space Administration [NASA], 2021). Imagine each molecule is a little ball in a bucket. If many balls are in a bucket and you shake the bucket, the balls move around. The balls form to the shape of the bucket, just like the molecules in water form to the shape of a cup. In contrast, in a solid such as a rock, the balls are "glued" together so they don't move around when you shake the bucket.

The Color of Water

Another important concept is the transparency of water. Clean, pure water in a bucket or glass has no color. We can see our fingers wiggle when we hold them under the surface. Yet, the color of water in the sea and in other natural bodies of water appears as blue. Water has unique properties that affect the ways it responds to light. Knowing that water is made up of molecules also helps us understand why clean water is transparent.

Ask a Water Scientist

Why does water have no color?

To explain why water seems to have no color, we need to first talk about the role of light in how we see colors. The color of a material is determined by how that material responds to the light that hits it. An object appears as a certain color because certain types of light that hit that object are absorbed by (taken in) or obstructed by (bounced off) that object. For example, a stop sign appears red because of the type of light that is reflected by (bounces off) the sign.

When light hits water, however, something different happens. As mentioned above, water is made up of tiny molecules. Water molecules have special properties that allow light to go straight through without getting reflected. These special properties of water molecules make the water look clear. This is why, when you observe water in a glass, it looks almost transparent (U.S. Geological Survey [USGS], 2018b).

Now you've expanded or reviewed your own content knowledge about water science. You know that water is made of molecules. You know that liquid water takes the shape of its container because its molecules are flowing and moving. You know that clean water is transparent because of how its molecules respond to light. While you won't be teaching these advanced concepts to preschool children, this knowledge will better equip you to facilitate conversations and activities that are related to the movement of water, the shape of water, and the color of water.

Explore

To spark curiosity about water, go straight to the source. If possible, give children the opportunity to observe and engage with water in the natural world. What options are available in your school's community? Are you near any bodies of water, such as lakes, rivers, ponds, or streams? Plan a walk or field trip that allows children to observe, hear, smell, and possibly touch water in a natural environment.

When visiting a body of water, tap into your own curiosity and delight in the beauty of the environment. You are an important role model for the children. Express your own excitement! Tell the children, "What an amazing lake. I love to watch the way the water moves toward the shoreline." Encourage children to observe the water by asking, "What do you see? What do you notice?"

If it's safe to do so, allow children to touch the water with their hands and notice how it feels on their fingers. If possible, have the children take off their shoes and socks and touch the water with their toes and feet.

If you're not able to visit a natural body of water, look for other options for observing the movement of water such as human-made waterways such as canals and gullies or even fountains. And look for opportunities to observe water after a rainfall in puddles or gutters.

Ask questions that encourage children to observe the movement of water and the color of water.

- How is the water moving?
- How do you know?
- What do you see?
- What do you hear?
- What do you feel?
- What do you smell?
- What are you wondering about how water moves?
- What questions do you have?

Document your experiences visiting and observing water in your community. Use a notebook or tablet to write down children's comments and questions. Take photos and ask the children to help you choose which views to capture. Record video of water moving. Invite children to actively participate in the documentation process by drawing what they see. Give them clipboards, paper, and pencils and invite them to sketch the way the water moves. You'll be able to use your documentation later to build play experiences and science activities that are based on their interests and questions.

Unfortunately, when visiting both natural and human-made bodies of water in your community, you and the children may notice garbage and litter in or near the water and other evidence that the water is not clean and safe. While disappointing to see, these are important observations too. In chapters 9 and 11, we'll explore activities that encourage children to notice and speak up about the importance of protecting our water and our environment.

Play

Open-ended exploratory play is crucial for children, as it encourages learning through direct interaction and experimentation. When children engage with water freely, they discover its characteristics through hands-on experience. Use the suggestions from chapter 1 to set up water play experiences indoors and outdoors.

Exploratory play with water engages the senses and motor skills, as children hold and manipulate objects, pour, and splash. The play ideas below include suggestions for materials and experiences that focus on the movement, shape, and color of water.

Container Play

During regular water play in sensory tables and bins, present children with containers of different sizes and shapes. This variety allows children to gain experience seeing how water moves when poured from one container to another and how an amount, or volume, of water looks when it takes on the shape of its container.

Vocabulary

Volume: the amount of space that is filled by a solid, liquid, or gas (Helmenstine, 2021)

To promote comparisons and problem-solving, present children with containers of contrasting sizes and shapes, such as a tall cup and a flat bowl. As mentioned in chapter 1, make sure the water play setting provides a flat surface where children can place the containers while they are pouring, such as a board that fits across the middle of a sensory table (see photo on p. 11) or, outdoors, the ledge of a sandbox.

Play with Funnels, Tubes, and Water Wheels

The addition of funnels, tubes, or water wheels provides new opportunities to experiment with how water moves when it pours, flows, or spills. Provide different shapes of funnels, along with containers, such as wide-mouthed bottles and vases, that will hold the funnels in place. Pouring water into the funnels requires some practice. Children will develop control and coordination through this type of play. They'll also begin to experiment to see how quickly or slowly water flows through different-sized funnels. They'll begin to learn that the shape of the funnel affects how quickly or slowly the water moves.

You can buy funnels from discount stores, kitchenware shops, and school supply companies, but you can also make your own funnels from plastic bottles. Instructions can be found online (for example, https://www.instructables.com/Funnel-from-plastic-bottle).

Incorporating plastic tubes into water play also encourages experimentation with the movement of water. Sets of toy tubes for water play are wonderful, but you can also fashion your own set from materials found at a hardware store, such as flexible plastic tubing and short segments of PVC pipes. Outdoors, where more space is available, rain gutter tubes and pool noodles (cut in half lengthwise) can be used to create water channels where children can plan, predict, and observe the flow of water.

Another great prop for observing the movement of water is a toy water wheel. A water wheel is a toy with a base that can stand hands-free and support a wheel with rotating paddles that turn freely when water flows over the paddles. To use a toy water wheel, children pour water into the top of the wheel using a cup or another container. The water flows over the paddles, causing the wheel to spin. Children can observe how the speed of the wheel changes depending on the amount or speed of the water flow. Children often enjoy experimenting with different ways of pouring water to see how it affects the wheel's movement.

Colored Water

As mentioned in chapter 1, teachers can add non-toxic dyes, such as food coloring or diluted watercolor paint, to the water in a sensory table or bin. Providing tinted water for water play adds novelty and interest to the children's experience. The color might inspire pretend play scenarios, such as creating a pretend ocean with blue water or creating a pretend lemonade stand with yellow water.

I've noticed that teachers often add the color in advance, before children begin playing. I recommend adding the color when children are present and can directly observe the transformation from clear, colorless water to tinted water. As you pour or drop the color into the water, don't stir it up right away. Take a moment to watch how the color slowly moves and mixes with the water. Children will observe the characteristics of water in motion as they see how the color flows and disperses through the liquid water.

If possible, invite children to take an active role in adding color. For example, prepare squeeze bottles with diluted colored water in advance and facilitate the taking of turns as each child adds a few drops of color to the sensory bin/table. The first few times you do this activity with children, stick to just one color. This will allow the children to see how the depth of color in the water changes as more dye or paint is added. After children have gained some experience with this process, introduce color mixing, in which children use two primary colors to create a secondary color—mixing yellow and red to make orange, blue and red to make purple, and yellow and blue to make green.

I recommend facilitating the adding and mixing of colors at the beginning of a free-play session, then allowing children plenty of time for open-ended free play with the colored water.

Mud Play

Most children enjoy playing outdoors with mud. Some playgrounds include features such as a mud kitchen equipped with a water source and cooking props that encourage mud play. Even without special equipment, children enjoy messing with mud.

The recipe for mud is simple: dirt plus water. Mud play, by definition, includes water play. When children can control the water sources—through a hose or a pump or a tap—they are able to experiment with the texture and consistency of the mud, a process that deepens the sensory experience and supports learning. Along with regular opportunities for water play indoors, mud play can be considered a core water science play experience.

Recommended Children's Books

***Water Is Water* by Miranda Paul**

Miranda Paul's nonfiction picture book describes examples of water throughout the water cycle and throughout the four seasons. The simple, poetic language presents the characteristics and properties of water in ways that are accessible to young children.

***Wave* by Suzy Lee**

This wordless picture book tells the story of child's day at the beach. The title of the book, as well as the images, draw attention to the movement of the water along the seashore. Wordless picture books such as *Wave* are best shared with children one-on-one and in small groups. Viewing and discussing the illustrations are the next best thing to a field trip to the beach.

***Water Rolls, Water Rises* by Pat Mora**

Pat Mora's lovely book visits water in motion all around the world. The simple, poetic text appears on each page in both English and Spanish.

Experiment

These teacher-facilitated science activities and experiments demonstrate key science concepts related to the characteristics of water.

Activity: Comparing Containers

When I observe children pouring water from one container to another, I'm reminded of Jean Piaget, the famous Swiss psychologist, and his theory of conservation. According to Piaget, a child's ability to *conserve*—to recognize, for example, that the volume of a liquid stays the same even when the size and shape of its container changes—demonstrates an important milestone

in the child's cognitive development (McLeod, 2024). For example, if you pour a certain quantity of water—say, 8 ounces—from a short, wide glass into a tall, thin glass, and ask a young child, "Which glass has more?" they may say the tall glass has more simply because the water level is higher. This type of mistake is not a concern; it is evidence of typical cognitive development in young children.

We can be intentional about providing children with opportunities to compare quantities of water in different containers by engaging children in some facilitated experiments with containers of contrasting shapes and sizes.

Prepare

Materials: several containers of contrasting shapes, such as a tall glass and a flat bowl; two pitchers or measuring cups with spouts

Ideally, choose containers that are clear and allow children to view the water level inside. Fill the two pitchers or measuring cups with the exact same amount of water. You might choose to add color to this water to ensure it will be clearly visible inside the containers.

Choose a quantity of water that will fit in each of the containers, with room to spare.

Observe and Experiment

I recommend that you have the children observe you demonstrating the experiment first, and then give them an opportunity to pour the water and make comparisons on their own.

First, show the children the two pitchers (or measuring cups) filled with water and ask them to compare them. Ask, "Are these the same amount of water or different? How do you know?"

Establish, through discussion and observation, that the amount of water is the same.

Demonstrate how to pour the water from one pitcher into the tall container and the water from the other pitcher into the flat container. Then ask, "Are these the same amount of water or different? How do you know?"

There's no need to correct children if they say the two amounts are different. The most important thing is the process. Ask children to explain their thinking.

Repeat the process as a demonstration or facilitate turn-taking among the children as they experiment with pouring and observing. If some of the water spills (which is likely!) be sure to re-measure the water to ensure that the amounts are the same in the two containers.

Document

Record children's comments, questions, and ideas by taking notes or making a video or audio recordings. Take photos that demonstrate how the two contrasting containers look, side by side. You can use this documentation later to facilitate discussion and reflection.

Reflect

Later, after everyone in the class has had a chance to try the experiment, gather children together to reflect on the experiment. If possible, show the children photos of the two contrasting containers. Invite discussion and reflection with open-ended questions such as:

- What did you think (predict) would happen when we poured the water?
- What did you notice?
- What did you wonder?
- What questions do you have about this science experiment?

Conducting simple science experiments like this are great opportunities to introduce scientific terms and processes, such as *science*, *experiment*, *predict*, and *observe*.

Think Ahead

The ideas and activities offered in this chapter are just the beginning of lifelong learning about water. Children are especially fascinated by how water moves, particularly outdoors in natural environments. The characteristics of water are new and exciting for young children. Practice looking at water with fresh eyes. We will expand and deepen our own curiosity as we continue to engage with children in play and science activities related to water. Observing and learning about the characteristics and properties of water, such as the behavior of liquids, will be especially helpful to both teachers and children when exploring topics related to weather and temperature. In the next two chapters, we will continue to build our water science content knowledge as we learn about water's starring role in weather (rain, snow, fog, and more) and explore some foundational ideas related to observing and measuring temperature.

Chapter Three:

Water and Weather

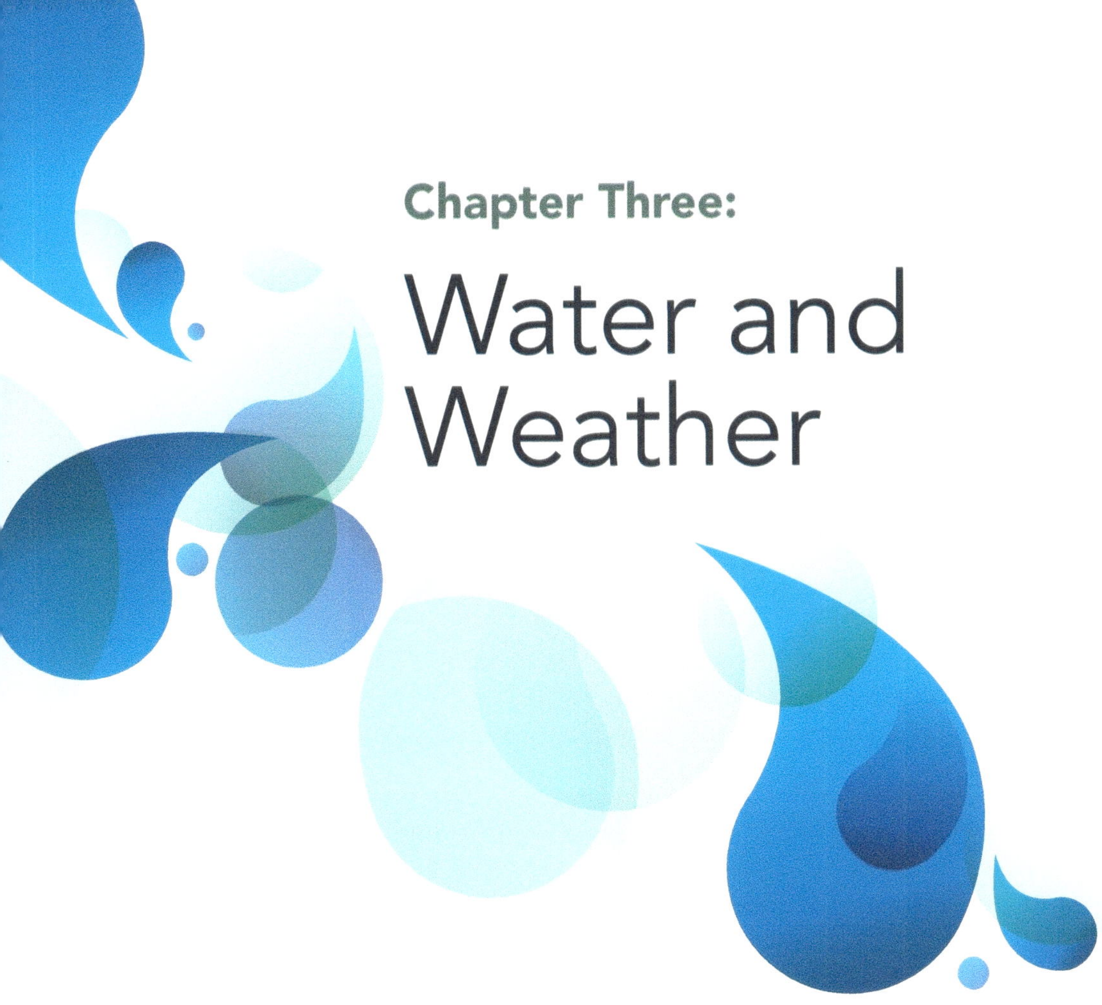

It's a Tuesday afternoon in Ms. Maria's and Ms. Sarah's preschool classroom. The teachers are helping the children clean up and get ready to play in the gym. Ordinarily, the class would be preparing to go outside, but the teachers checked the weather report earlier, and they know it's too rainy to go outside.

Just as the children are starting to line up at the door, a loud rumble of thunder is heard from outside. A few children run to the windows to look out while a few others start to cry.

"I heard some thunder," says Ms. Maria in a calm voice.

"I heard it too," said Ms. Sarah. "I think some of us were surprised by that loud sound." Several children nod and say, "I was surprised!"

After a second rumble of thunder, the teachers decide to bring the children back to the rug to sit down and talk about what's happening.

Ms. Maria says, "Let's rest on the rug for a minute until everyone feels ready to go to the gym. It sounds like some children are worried about the weather."

Ms. Sarah says, "Sometimes, when it's rainy, the clouds make a sound called thunder. It can be a loud sound. But the thunder can't hurt us. We are all safe here inside."

> Ms. Maria asks the children, "What do you know about thunder?"
>
> Several children raise their hands. Ms. Maria calls on Henry. "I know about lightning! It makes a big flash and boom!"
>
> "Yes," says Ms. Maria. "Lightning is a bright flash of light. It can happen during a storm."
>
> The children continue sharing what they know about thunder, lightning, and storms. Then Ms. Maria asks, "Does anyone have questions about the weather?"
>
> One child asks, "Where is the thunder?"
>
> Another child asks, "Who makes the lightning?"
>
> Ms. Sarah writes down the children's questions.
>
> After a few minutes, the teachers decide it's time to head to the gym. Ms. Sarah says to Ms. Maria, "It seems like the children have a lot of questions about weather. Let's be sure to come back to these questions and ideas another time."

As this vignette illustrates, young children are often aware of the weather in their environment, especially when there are dramatic changes such as storms. One of our important jobs as educators is helping children understand the things that surprise or frighten them. Teaching and learning about the weather (and about the role of water in weather phenomena) support that process.

The Importance of Water and Weather

Ever notice how people love to talk about the weather? Strangers chat about the weather at bus stops. Forecasters share their predictions on apps, on the radio, and on television. Rain or shine, warm or cold, everyone has something to say about the weather.

Weather is part of everyone's lives, and water is part of every kind of weather. Water plays a starring role in all kinds of precipitation, from rain to snow to fog to sleet. Sometimes, the weather brings us too much water, and at other times, the weather is too dry and we look to the skies, hoping for rain.

Children recognize at a very young age that water and weather are essential parts of our daily lives. Learning about water and weather is meaningful to children because these are topics that have a visible impact on their families and the people they care about. Children hear adults talk about the weather and, more importantly, they directly experience the weather each day with all their senses. Children feel a splash of rain on their skin, the chill of a strong wind at their backs, and the warm caress of the sun on their faces.

Concerns about Weather and Climate Change

Weather is a powerful force in our lives that can stir up strong feelings of hope, gratitude, and awe, as well as helplessness, anxiety, and fear. Extreme weather events such as hurricanes, floods, and snowstorms can inspire concern about our safety. Climate scientists tell us that extreme weather events may become more intense and more frequent in the future due to climate change. This apprehension about a future impacted by climate change can influence our mental health. For example, the American Psychological Association now describes a condition called *ecoanxiety,* "a chronic fear of environmental doom" that causes a range of responses from mild stress to clinical disorders such as depression (Whitmore-Williams, Manning, Krygsman, and Speiser, 2017) and can often be linked to extreme weather events. While there's not yet research to tell us how ecoanxiety might impact young children, we can draw some conclusions from what we already know about child development. We know that children are affected when their parents and caregivers feel stress. We also know that children are influenced by what they see and hear in the media. They may not understand the news and current events, but they can often tell when something scary has happened or might be about to happen. For example, in the aftermath of Hurricane Helene, which caused severe flooding in North Carolina in the fall of 2024, children and families throughout the state were directly and indirectly impacted by hardships such as power outages and road and school closures for months after the event (Vespa, 2024).

What can we, as early childhood professionals, do to help support young children who might be affected by the stress of climate change and extreme weather events? One clear, positive step is to teach children developmentally appropriate concepts about water and weather so they can learn to understand weather and, in small ways, take some control of weather's effects on their lives. And we can do this every day in the context of children's direct experiences with water and weather day to day.

Learning Objectives

The NGSS offers learning objectives specific to water and weather:

Next Generation Science Standards

K-ESS2 Earth's Systems

Students who demonstrate understanding can:

K-ESS2-1 use and share observations of local weather conditions to describe patterns over time (National Research Council, 2013).

Additionally, NGSS includes the topic of weather and climate among the disciplinary core ideas:

> **ESS2.D** Weather and Climate
>
> Weather is a combination of sunlight, wind, snow or rain, and temperature in a particular region at a particular time. People measure these conditions to describe and record the weather and to notice patterns over time (National Research Council, 2013).

Weather is another water science topic that is specifically mentioned as key content in the NAEYC (2022) accreditation standards under Topic 2.G Science.

The following learning objectives are informed by the NGSS and NAEYC accreditation standards as described above, as well as by the Head Start Early Learning Outcomes Framework and current research in the field of child development and science education. The four objectives are worded and structured in ways that help you scaffold children's learning experiences, provide meaningful, play-based contexts for learning, and create foundations for future learning.

Chapter 3 Learning Objectives

1. Support children's growing understanding of weather phenomena.
2. Provide opportunities for children to observe and discuss their observations and sensory experiences related to weather.
3. Expose children to concepts related to the weather such as precipitation and temperature during regular water play indoors and outdoors.
4. Conduct teacher-facilitated science activities and experiments that demonstrate weather concepts.

Background Information for Educators

As early childhood educators, we need to know a little bit about water and weather as we lead and facilitate learning in our classrooms. But we don't need to have a degree in meteorology to understand that water is an essential part of weather. A helpful starting point is simply an understanding of the definition of *weather* as the combination of sunlight, wind, snow or rain, and temperature in a particular region at a particular time (National Research Council, 2013). Beyond that, much of our own learning and discovery about weather can happen side by side with the children as we follow their emerging interests and our own authentic sense of curiosity.

Climate scientists remind us, however, that *weather* and *climate* are not exactly the same thing. It can be helpful to know the difference between these two terms and use them correctly in our work with children. As noted above, *weather* refers to the conditions at a particular time and place. *Climate*, on the other hand, refers to the patterns of weather conditions over a longer period of time in a particular region. In other words, *weather* refers to the here and now—what's happening outside your window. *Climate* is a much broader concept and refers to patterns and trends over time in a larger area. In Chicago, for example, the climate in January is cold and snowy. We know this because of the broad trends in this part of the country. However, the specific weather on a particular day in January might be sunny and above freezing. Weather can change significantly from day to day, but climate refers to patterns over time that tell us what we might expect in a particular area, in this case Chicago.

Vocabulary

Blizzard: a severe snowstorm with strong, cold winds

Climate: the usual or average weather conditions in a particular place or region measured over a long period of time

Flood: a large amount of water rising over an area of land that is usually dry

Hurricane: an extremely large and powerful storm system with strong winds

Ice: water that is frozen

Lightning: the flashes of light in the sky, often during a storm, caused by atmospheric electricity

Precipitation: snow, hail, sleet, rain, or mist

Rain: water that falls in drops from the sky

Sleet: frozen rain

Snow: small, white ice crystals that fall from the sky in cold weather

Snowstorm: a weather system with a large amount of snow

Storm: a weather occurrence marked by strong winds and often including heavy rain or snow

Thunder: the loud sound that follows a flash of lightning during a storm

Tornado: a whirling, destructive wind that moves in a narrow path over land

Weather: the conditions of the atmosphere at a particular time and place with respect to temperature and precipitation

Explore

Educators inspired by the schools of Reggio Emilia, Italy, talk about invitations to learning as provocations. I find a lot of value in thinking intentionally about how to provoke or spark children's interest in a new topic and, in this case, inspire curiosity about weather. Among the most meaningful ways to inspire children to explore the weather is through direct experience outdoors.

Experience the Weather Outdoors

All of us, both adults and children, probably notice the weather at some level of awareness when we are outdoors. But if our intent is to inspire or provoke new excitement for learning about weather, we can take a cue from the practices of mindfulness and meditation by inviting children to be still and present, using our senses to observe and experience the weather.

This type of invitation is best presented to children after they have already had time for active outdoor play. As we all know, young children need to move and exercise their bodies. Daily outdoor play is essential to any early childhood program. But before the children come inside, when they are ready for a moment of rest, invite the children to stand, sit, or even lie down outdoors and use their senses to experience the weather.

Ask children questions such as:

- What's the weather like today?
- How do you know?
- What do you see?
- What do you hear?
- What do you feel?
- What do you smell?
- What are you wondering about the weather?
- What questions do you have?

The first time you invite children to experience the weather in this way, they might have trouble slowing down and tuning in to the sights, sounds, and sensations that are related to the weather. Don't give up! Try again and, if possible, makes these moments a routine "wind down" after active play. You might give this practice a name, such as "weather time" or "noticing time."

Document children's observations and behavior during this time. Use a notebook or tablet to write down children's comments and questions. Take photos or video. Invite children to actively participate in the documentation process. Give them clipboards, paper, and pencils and ask them to draw what they see in the sky or sketch the way the wind moves the branches of a tree. You'll be able to use this information later to build play experiences and science activities that are based on their interests and questions.

Bring the Weather Inside

Another way to invite or provoke interest in the weather is to observe the weather from indoors, through a window or open doorway. Again, the same questions can be used to invite children's ideas.

- What's the weather like today?
- How do you know?

- What do you see?
- What do you hear?
- What do you feel?
- What do you smell?
- What are you wondering about the weather?
- What questions do you have?

These observations and conversations could be practiced as a full class or in small groups. If the classroom space allows for a group of chairs or pillows to be placed near a window, this space could become a special weather observation station, with clipboards and paper set aside for observations and documentation.

A Note About Weather Charts

Daily calendar time is a common practice in many early childhood classrooms, and sometimes these calendar rituals include checking the weather. For example, during calendar time, a teacher may ask a child to take a turn looking out the window and giving the class a weather report or perhaps placing a weather symbol (such as a cardboard sun, cloud, raindrop, or snowflake) on the calendar. In my experience, this type of daily weather checking does not give the children enough time to be able to truly observe the weather and take note of the many fascinating and sometimes subtle variations in the weather from day to day or even from hour to hour. For example, a cardboard cloud symbol doesn't accurately represent the many variations in the colors of the clouds or in the texture of the clouds. A brief peek out the window isn't enough time to observe the movement of the clouds and the many different ways the wind might be moving the clouds across the sky. As Erika Christakis (2017) writes in her book *The Importance of Being Little*, "Calendar activities consume an enormous amount of a teacher's time even though there are more effective ways to help a young child learn...." I agree and suggest that the time spent in calendar time would be better spent simply looking out the window watching the sky, or, better yet, spent outdoors with nothing but the sky over our heads.

Play

The most exciting, complex, and creative learning takes place during open-ended exploratory play (Zosh et al., 2017). Although free-choice play is child directed, teachers can still support and facilitate learning by providing time, space, materials, and provocations that allow children to explore and deepen their understandings of water and weather.

Sensory Play

As noted previously, children's direct sensory experiences with weather and water in the natural world inspire the richest and most exciting learning. Play in which children freely explore weather and water can take place on playgrounds, in parks, on neighborhood walks, and during special excursions and field trips.

One of the most obvious and direct connections between water and weather is the phenomenon of rain. Rain can be experienced as it falls from the sky, and, afterward, the evidence of rain is found in puddles and mud.

Ideally, children come to school dressed in clothing that is suitable for playing in puddles of water and exploring wet, muddy soil. Some early childhood programs provide protective clothing such as waterproof boots, slickers, and all-weather coveralls. In some circumstances, if adults have checked the area for hazards and the temperature is warm enough, children may be allowed to play barefoot in puddles and mud, especially if they can be easily washed off in a hose or a sprinkler afterward.

The same can be said of playing in the snow. With the proper clothing that provides protection from the cold, most children love playing in the snow. It is the direct sensory experience of touching and playing with the rain and snow that the children will learn the characteristics and properties of liquid and frozen water.

Teachers can also bring rain and snow indoors for exploratory sensory play. Rainwater can be collected in rain barrels or buckets and placed in sensory tables or bins. Children can use sieves or slotted spoons to fish out leaves or other items that might be mixed with rain outdoors. Snow, too, can be brought indoors for play. Play with snow must begin right away, before it melts too much! Children may prefer to play with snow while wearing mittens or gloves to protect their fingers from the cold.

Other weather phenomena can be simulated indoors. Wind, for example, can be simulated in the classroom using an electric fan. For safety, make sure the slats or openings on the fan are too narrow to allow children's fingers to get inside, or cover the fan with a mesh screen. Once the fan is turned on, invite children to play with lightweight items such as feathers, balloons, or streamers, and invite children to notice how the movement of air impacts the movement of the play items.

Pretend Play

Many preschool classrooms have space set aside for pretend play, with housekeeping equipment and other kinds of dramatic play props. Adding elements of weather to the play settings can inspire children to build pretend play scenarios around different kinds of weather phenomena.

For example, add weather-related props to the dramatic play materials such as:

- umbrellas
- rain hats
- rain boots
- cold weather hats and scarves
- mittens
- small snow shovels or ice scrapers
- sunglasses
- sun hats
- goggles

Consider adding weather elements to children's indoor play using audio or video recordings of different kinds of weather conditions. For example, use a projector to show a video of rainy weather on the wall of the classroom or play an audio recording of a gentle rainstorm. Many meditation apps include ambient sounds of rain or wind. These visual and auditory additions to the free-play environment can be a wonderful source of curiosity and inspiration for child-directed sensory and pretend play.

Recommended Children's Books

It's wonderful to see how the picture books we read aloud to children influence their pretend play. Sharing picture books about the water and weather often sparks creative play scenarios related to weather phenomena. Some of my favorite picture books about the weather include:

***When the Storm Comes* by Linda Ashman**

This is one of my favorite weather picture books because the words and illustrations demonstrate how people and animals prepare for storms in a way that is both accurate and reassuring.

***I Face the Wind* by Vicki Cobb**

Vicki Cobb's *I Face the Wind* is part of a series of science books targeted for a very young audience. The explanations and illustrations of the phenomenon of wind are simple and direct.

***I Am a Tornado* by Drew Beckmeyer**

I Am a Tornado is a fun mix of science and fiction. Of course, tornados can't talk to cows, but if they did, Drew Beckmeyer's book shows exactly what they might say. The story includes some factual information about the weather conditions that cause tornados, but the real value of this read aloud is how it demonstrates the management of big feelings.

***I Feel Safe* by David McPhail**

This comforting picture book tells the story of a child with an extended family and their experience during a thunderstorm. The adults find ways to help everyone feel safe even when the electricity goes out.

Experiment

As discussed earlier, observation and documentation are important parts of scientific learning. Other important processes include using tools, such as thermometers and rain gauges, making predictions, recognizing patterns, and observing cause and effect. The science experiments suggested here support these processes. Unlike the open-ended and child-directed play activities described earlier in this chapter, these experiments are facilitated by a teacher, with plenty of opportunities for children's active participation. Some elements of these activities can be introduced during large-group class sessions, but the most active experimentation is best conducted during small-group time or as a center choice during free play.

Activity: Measure Precipitation

There are many different ways that children can participate in the measuring of both liquid precipitation (rain) and solid precipitation (snow). During rainy weather, a rain gauge—a clear,

open container with measurement markings—can be placed outdoors to collect rainwater. Rain gauges can be purchased online or at home improvement stores. But any clear, open container could be used as a rain gauge. You could add measurement marks (inch or centimeter) to the side of the container using permanent marker. Or you could help the children use a ruler, placed next to a plain container, to measure the quantity (height) of rain in the container.

Similarly, for measuring snowfall, a ruler could be placed outdoors in a space where snow is expected to accumulate. Children can participate in placing the ruler and in observing and recording the results.

Children can also be encouraged to use nonstandard units of measurement to observe the quantity of rain or snow. For example, you can choose a landmark on a playground, such as slide, and children can be guided to observe and count how many steps on the ladder are covered after a heavy snowfall.

Young children in preschool and kindergarten are still learning math concepts about numeracy and measurement. The primary objective of these activities is to demonstrate and observe the varying levels of precipitation at any given time. Sometimes, it rains a lot. Sometimes, it rains just a little. But how do we know? We can measure precipitation such as rain and snow in many different ways. Children can also be invited to come up with their own ideas for measuring precipitation.

Prepare

For measuring rain, purchase or create a rain gauge. At group time, show the children the gauge and explain its purpose. Pass the gauge around the circle and give everyone a chance to hold it and study it. Invite the children to share their ideas for where we should place the rain gauge. Document children's ideas and questions.

For measuring snow, prepare a ruler or yardstick, or identify a few possible landmarks or objects that might be used as nonstandard measuring tools.

Observe and Experiment

Once the rain gauge is placed outdoors, encourage children to check regularly for evidence of rain. If a rainy spell occurs right away, make a plan for the children to go outdoors after the rain is over and observe the rain gauge. If possible, carry the gauge inside and place it where children can observe it closely. Put out paper and pencils so the children can draw or write what they see. If days pass without rain, invite children to document how many days pass before they observe any rain in the rain gauge.

If you have access to a portable/remote security camera, you can provide a real-time opportunity for children to observe your rain gauge or snow measurement tool. Point the camera so the gauge or tool is easily visible. Many digital security cameras come with an app that allows you to view the live feed from a tablet or smart phone. This would allow the children to observe the measuring tools during a precipitation event, even when it's too rainy or snowy to go outside.

Document

Create documentation of children's explorations and experiments with measuring rain and snow. This type of activity is best repeated over time so children can make predictions and comparisons. Post photos and labels of the rain gauge in the classroom so children can remember the varying results over time.

Reflect

Measuring precipitation in combination with other weather and water activities can help children make connections between different ideas and experiences. For example, invite children to play with rain gauges (or similarly shaped containers) during water play in a sensory bin or table. On a rainy day, read a picture book about rain (such as *When the Storm Comes*) before or after checking the rain gauge.

Activity: Monitor the Temperature

As noted in the previous activity, young children are still learning the math concepts necessary to fully understand how to use measuring tools, such as a thermometer. But children can explore the differences and variations of warm and cold weather and they can begin to understand that a temperature can be *high* or *higher* when it's warm, and *low* or *lower* when it's cold.

Prepare

Materials: non-breakable, child-safe thermometers for use with people, food, and air

Collect a variety of non-breakable thermometers that are safe for children to touch and explore in a small group with teacher facilitation. For example, many children are already familiar with the type of thermometer used to measure body temperature, such as the digital thermometers used under the arm or under a tongue or the infrared thermometers used on a forehead. These thermometers can be used as an introduction to these activities and source of reference for the kinds of thermometers used to measure air temperature.

There are many different kinds of weather thermometers or air thermometers, such as digital thermometers and dial thermometers. Avoid using glass-tube mercury thermometers with children as both the glass and the mercury can be hazardous. However, some science-supply and school-supply companies sell plastic tube thermometers with a red liquid that is mercury-free. These student-friendly thermometers are good for helping children make the connection between a high temperature and a low temperature because the red line moves higher for high temperatures and lower for low temperatures.

Observe and Experiment

Introduce the thermometer collection as a small-group activity. First, show the children the body temperature thermometers and ask them what they already know about these tools. Take note of their responses on a chart or notebook. If possible, allow the children to hold and use the thermometers (with teacher support and facilitation).

Next, build on what children already know and ask, "We know how to measure the temperature of our bodies, but how can we measure the temperature of the air outside?" Invite their responses and document their ideas. Then show the children a few of the other types of thermometers and invite them to think about which one(s) might be best for measuring the air temperature outside.

After all the children have had a turn in the small group, invite the class to make some decisions together about which thermometers you will use outdoors.

Decide with the children where you might place the thermometers outside.

Once the thermometers are in place, create a class plan for monitoring and reading the temperatures each day and perhaps at different times of day.

Document

A bar graph is a great way to document temperature over time. Young children can easily see and understand that some temperature measurements are higher and some are lower. Create a graph on a large piece of paper or bulletin board.

Facilitate regular graphing sessions where children take turns recording the temperature on the graph. Children could color in squares on the bar, or they could add a certain number of shape stickers to create a bar on the bar graph.

Reflect

Maintain the graphing activity for several days to allow children the opportunity to observe and compare the temperature over a period of time. This activity could be combined with measuring precipitation, and children could be invited to consider connections or relationships between temperature and precipitation.

Weather-Related Resources

Weather Sounds

Audio Library: Weather-Sound Effects on YouTube
https://www.youtube.com/playlist?list=PL4JKIH8uMAXxeUWlZT1ZlLu-ppUJL7Pty

"Rainfall on Forest Foliage"
https://www.youtube.com/watch?v=vKx40e7LX7g

"Relaxing Snowfall"
https://www.youtube.com/watch?v=vz91QpgUjFc

Sound Effects! App
https://apps.apple.com/us/app/sound-effects/id542839600

Real-Time Weather Videos

National Weather Service Weather Cameras
https://www.weather.gov/gjt/weathercameras

Federal Aviation Administration Weather Cams
https://weathercams.faa.gov/

Teacher Resources

National Oceanic and Atmospheric Administration, Educational Resources
https://www.noaa.gov/educational-resources

Think Ahead

Children's experiences with weather often lead to conversations about temperature. In the next chapter, we'll explore activities, stories, and conversations that build on children's understanding of temperature using thermometers.

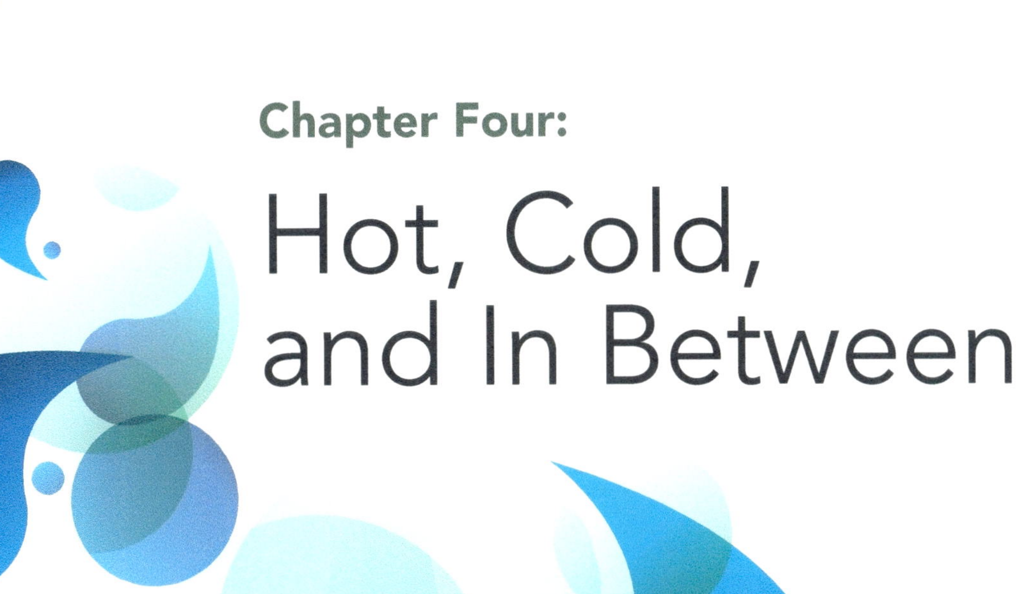

Chapter Four:

Hot, Cold, and In Between

Two preschool children, Lola and Trey, are getting ready to wash their hands at a single sink in the school bathroom. Lola is four and has been enrolled at the school for several months, but Trey, age three, is new.

Their teacher, Ms. Nell, stands nearby.

"It's Lola's turn to wash," Ms. Nell says. "You're next, Trey."

Lola turns on the warm water on the left side of the sink and puts her hands under the stream of water coming from the fountain. The sink has one faucet but two separate handles, one to control the warm water and one to control the cold water. Ms. Nell knows that the water temperature for the whole facility is controlled so that the water will not go above 120 degrees, even if the warm water runs for a long time. She allows each child to choose whether they prefer to run the warm water, the cold water, or both.

Lola quickly washes with soap, rinses, and starts to dry her hands on a paper towel. Meanwhile, Trey steps up to the sink and puts his hands under the faucet. "Too hot!" says Trey, pulling his hands away from the stream of water.

"Is that water too warm for you, Trey?" asks Ms. Nell.

Trey nods.

Ms. Nell says, "It is warm water but not too hot. It won't burn you."

Trey stands at the sink watching the water come out of the faucet, but he does not put his hands into the water.

Ms. Nell says, "Some people like the way the warm water feels on their fingers. Other people like cooler water."

Lola, drying her hands, says, "Trey, you can turn off the warm water and turn on the cold water." She adds, "I'll show you how."

Lola pushes the handle on the warm water to turn it off. Then she turns the other handle and cool water begins to flow from the faucet.

"See?" says Lola.

Trey begins washing his hands. Lola says, "I like warm water and you like cold water."

As demonstrated in this vignette, handwashing is a time when children are directly engaged in a sensory experience that demonstrates the concept of temperature in relation to water. Even if young children don't know the word *temperature* or have any experience with a thermometer, they can still sense the difference between warm and cold when the water touches their skin. These experiences with water help build a foundation of understanding that will inform children's later learning about science. For example, in elementary school children will likely learn about the states of matter including liquid, solids, and gas. Temperature, of course, is one of the most essential factors in determining the state of water.

In my experience as an early childhood educator, I've observed that children are often fascinated by the concept of ice. (I think the popularity of a certain Disney movie probably has something to do with that!) But some of my earliest childhood memories are from the cold November days when the surface of the puddles on the sidewalk would freeze and we children could walk over the puddles, listening to the *crick-crack* of broken ice and watching the lines of thin cracks spread beneath our feet.

This chapter builds on both children's natural curiosity about temperature, how temperature affects their daily routines, the foods they eat, and the weather they observe. The science concepts in this chapter build on concepts described in the previous chapters of this book and also relate to the concept of the water cycle that will be addressed in chapter 10.

Learning Objectives

This chapter addresses concepts related to observing and measuring the temperature of water and builds on concepts related to states of matter (liquid, solid) introduced in chapter 2. Guidance on teaching children to use authentic scientific tools, such as thermometers, is also included. As discussed in the introduction of this book, the Head Start Early Learning Outcomes Framework affirms the importance of exploring water science in preschool. Additionally, the Head Start framework specifically refers to the value of using measurement tools such as thermometers.

Head Start Early Learning Outcomes Framework

Domain: Scientific Reasoning

Sub-Domain: Reasoning and Problem-Solving

Goal P-SCI 3. Child compares and categorizes observable phenomena.

Indicators (by 60 Months)

Uses measurement tools, such as a ruler, balance scale, eye dropper, unit blocks, thermometer, or measuring cup, to quantify similarities and differences of observable phenomena (U.S. Department of Health and Human Services, Administration for Children and Families, Office of Head Start, 2015).

Similarly, NAEYC Accreditation Standards refers to the "simple tools" as one of the important methods for supporting children's scientific inquiry and knowledge.

NAEYC Early Learning Program Accreditation Standards and Assessment Items

Topic 2.G

Shares ideas and recommendations for activities that support children's scientific inquiry (NAEYC, 2022).

Based on the Head Start framework, NAEYC accreditation standards, and other sources, the following learning objectives can help frame and inform our teaching and learning about water concepts and phenomena that are related to temperature. The four objectives are worded and structured in ways that help you scaffold children's learning experiences, provide meaningful, play-based contexts for learning, and create foundations for future learning.

Chapter 4 Learning Objectives

1. Support children's growing understanding of the properties of matter and temperature, in particular the differences between liquid water and ice.
2. Provide opportunities for children to observe and discuss the differences between liquid water and ice.
3. During regular water play indoors and outdoors, expose children to safe sensory experiences that allow children to explore and discover the properties of water.
4. Conduct teacher-facilitated science activities experiments that demonstrate the uses of thermometers.

Background Information for Educators

You probably already know how to use a thermometer, and you understand that higher temperatures are hotter and lower temperatures are cooler. Here are a few additional explanations and facts related to measuring the temperature of water that might be helpful to you as an early childhood educator.

What Is Temperature?

Temperature is a measurement that indicates how hot or cold something is. When we are measuring the temperature of water, we are actually measuring the kinetic energy in the particles of water. The faster the particles are moving, the greater the energy and the higher the temperature. If the movement of particles slows, the temperature drops. We can intuitively understand the relationship between movement and heat because humans usually feel warmer when we move and exercise and feel cooler when we sit still (American Chemical Society, 2024).

How Do We Measure Temperature?

We don't always need a thermometer to learn important information about temperature. Sometimes, we can measure the *relative* temperature of a substance, such as water or air, simply by touch. When you take a sip of water, you can feel (and taste) whether the water feels warm or cool. This temperature is relative because you are sensing whether the water is warm or cool as compared to the temperature of your own body.

The most accurate way to measure temperature is with a thermometer. There are three temperature scales: Fahrenheit (°F), Celsius (°C), and Kelvin (K). Fahrenheit is primarily used in the United States, and Celsius is used in countries outside the United States. Kelvin is a special scale used by scientists. Later in this chapter, we'll explain some of the different kinds of thermometers and their potential uses in an early childhood classroom.

What Are States of Matter?

The scientific concept of states of matter is closely related to temperature and the movement of particles. The states of matter include liquids, solids, and gasses. (There are other states of matter such as plasma, but we don't need to address that here.) As discussed in chapter 2, a *liquid* is a substance that is able to flow freely. The molecules in liquid water move freely and conform to the shape of its container. In contrast, the molecules in a solid don't move much. A *solid*, such as frozen water (also known as ice) has a definite shape. As the temperature of a liquid decreases, its molecules move slower and slower until they stop, and the substance is then in solid form (Bagley, 2023). For water, this happens at 32 degrees Fahrenheit. The molecules in a gas, however, move a lot! A gas has no shape or form. As the temperature of a liquid increases its molecules move faster and faster until they become a gas. For water, this happens at 212 degrees Fahrenheit.

Vocabulary

Temperature: a degree of measurement that tells how hot or cold something is

Liquid: a substance that can flow freely

Solid: a substance that is not a gas or a liquid and cannot flow freely

Gas: a substance (such as steam) that has no fixed shape and tends to expand

Ask a Water Scientist

In a house, apartment, or school building, what makes the cold water cold and hot water hot?

What about in nature? Why is the water in streams and lakes usually so much cooler than the air temperature?

Water from faucets in buildings such as an apartment, a house, or a school can come out as hot or cold. Water is transported to these buildings through pipes that are usually underground where the temperature is cool. For hot water, a water heater is used to warm up the water before it comes out of your tap. Otherwise, you get the naturally cold water.

Water temperatures in nature, such as a lake or river, are controlled by a property of water called heat capacity. Heat capacity describes how easily a material can heat up. The heat capacity of water is very high, meaning that it takes a lot of energy to heat water up. Energy in the natural environment comes in the form of sunlight. Air has a much lower heat capacity, so it's easier for air to heat up. When the weather is sunny, the air temperature will increase much faster than water temperatures, which is why lakes and rivers are cooler than the air.

Explore

Most young children experience varying temperatures of water, air, and other materials as part of their daily lives. Here are a few ideas for drawing children's attention to temperature through scientific phenomena. You can use these experiences to spark conversations, questions, and curiosity that you can use to build play experiences and design teacher-facilitated science experiments.

Explore the Contrast of Warm and Cold

Many conversations and explorations about temperature can happen without a thermometer. We can use our senses to explore concepts of temperature as we notice contrasts between and changes in temperatures.

Washing Hands

As demonstrated in the vignette at the start of the chapter, handwashing is a time when children directly experience the sensations of warm or cold water on their skin. Ideally, allow children some supervised opportunities (within reason) to experiment with manipulating the handles that control the flow of water from the faucet into the sink. This is how they'll learn to become more independent in their ability to use the sinks and to recognize how to adjust the temperature of the water flowing onto their hands.

Eating Food and Drinking Liquids

Meals are another wonderful opportunity to explore and discuss sensory experiences related to temperature. If both warm and cold foods are served at the same meal, ask children to talk about what they feel and taste. For example, if the children are served warm soup and cold fruit, ask, "What do you notice about this food? How are these foods different from each other?" If a child comments on the temperature, ask, "How do you know?" Encourage children to really notice the feeling of warmth or coolness on their tongue and in their throat.

Experiencing the Weather

As described in the previous chapter, experiencing the weather outdoors can be a full sensory experience. When children step outside and feel a cool wind on their faces, engage in conversation about this scientific phenomenon. "What's the weather like today? How do you know? How does the air feel on your skin?"

Observe and Explore Ice

If you're fortunate enough to live in a climate where puddles freeze, snow falls, and icicles form, these are excellent opportunities to explore concepts of temperature and water science. (Children and teachers who live in warmer climates can experience ice in the sensory table; see "Play with Ice" on page 53.)

Frozen Puddles

I mentioned in the chapter introduction that I loved walking on frozen puddles when I was a child. Exploring frozen puddles on a sidewalk is best done first thing in the morning, after a hard freeze overnight. The best frozen puddles are the ones that are just crusted with ice on the surface, with liquid water beneath. The surface ice will usually make a satisfying cracking sound when it breaks, and you can observe a fascinating mix of delicate cracks as well as air bubbles beneath the surface. Keep in mind that ice is a slippery surface, and teach the children to step carefully. If the puddle is too deep or too slick to safely step on, show the children how to use a stick or rock to break the surface of the ice. Talk about what you see and, if possible, take pictures or video to revisit later.

Snow

There are few pleasures in life more exciting and inspiring than a fresh blanket of snow that turns the landscape into a winter wonderland. Most children are eager to explore snow through open ended play—walking and running through the snow, holding and shaping the snow, sweeping and shoveling snow, collecting snow in buckets and other containers, and more. Beyond ensuring that children are safely bundled up and appropriately dressed, there's not much teachers need to do on a snowy day to provide a complex sensory experience that demonstrates the characteristics of frozen water in the form of snow.

To extend the experience indoors, here are some recommended picture books about snow:

- *Curious About Snow* by Gina Shaw
- *The Snowy Day* by Ezra Jack Keats
- *Little Owl's Snow* by Divya Srinivasan
- *Ten Ways to Hear Snow* by Cathy Camper
- *Snowflake Bentley* by Jacqueline Briggs Martin

Icicles

If you and the children happen upon icicles as part of your frozen explorations, consider yourself lucky. Observing icicles is a fantastic opportunity to observe a scientific phenomenon and to think and talk about how liquid water turns to ice. If possible, observe the icicles in the same position where they formed, without breaking them, and ask the children, "Where did the icicles come from? How did they form?" Guide children in observing any dripping water or noticing any sources of liquid water that might have helped form the icicles. Ask the children to make prediction about what will happen next. "Will the icicles get bigger, or will they melt?" Check back later and see if the predictions came true.

Play

Safely exploring hot water and steam is not possible in an early childhood classroom, even with adult supervision. It's better to focus our explorations of temperature on the fascinating phenomenon of ice.

Play with Ice

Indoors, add ice to water play in sensory tables or sensory bins. Here are a few options:

- **Ice cubes or crushed ice:** Most of us have access to ice each day in our freezers, as cubes or crushed ice. Adding ice cubes or crushed ice to the water during regular water play creates a new sensory element to the children's experience. Be sure to add the ice while children are present so they can observe and feel the ice before it begins to melt.
- **Solid blocks of ice (icebergs):** A big piece of ice might spark some interesting conversations and creative pretend play. A few blocks of ice can be created in advance by pouring water into a few clean plastic carryout containers. The shapes might be round, square, or oval. Then float these blocks of ice in the water during sensory play. Add a few plastic toy sea creatures, and penguins or polar bears, and you've got an Arctic (North Pole) or Antarctic (South Pole) ecosystem.
- **Other ice shapes:** Party stores and kitchen supply stores often sell ice cube trays that create ice in novelty shapes, such as stars or hearts. These unique ice cubes can add a new and exciting element to water play. You can also add a little food coloring to the water before freezing.

- **Real snow:** Bring the outdoors inside by filling your sensory tables and bins with real snow. (Children may prefer to wear gloves or mittens for this type of activity.) When you collect the snow outdoors, make sure the snow is clean and untouched by people or animals.

Recommended Children's Books

***Best in Snow* by April Pulley Sayre**

In *Best in Snow*, beautiful photo illustrations demonstrate the winter weather cycle.

***Freezing and Melting* by Robin Nelson**

This is a rare find—a nonfiction science book with developmentally appropriate explanations of water phenomena. The simple text and photographs explain how water changes from a solid to a liquid and back again.

***Should I Share My Ice Cream?* by Mo Willems**

Elephant isn't sure if he should share his ice cream with his friend Piggie. He spends so much time deciding that his ice cream melts. This humorous story provides a fun example of the concept of temperature and the contrast between warm and cold.

Experiment

Activity: Practice Using Thermometers

A thermometer is a simple tool that provides essential information about the temperature of air, water, and other materials. With adult support, young children can learn to safely hold and use different kinds of thermometers.

Prepare

Materials: child-safe thermometers

The best kind of thermometer to use with children is one that is safe and easy to read. Thermometers made of glass are too fragile for an early childhood classroom, and thermometers made with mercury should never be used near children, even under adult supervision. Mercury is considered a poison, and spilled mercury from a broken thermometer creates a significant health hazard.

Fortunately, there are a wide variety of thermometers available that do not use mercury. Digital thermometers show the temperature with numerals on a screen. Analog thermometers show the temperature as a vertical (non-mercury) red line or as a dial on a circle face. I prefer using analog classroom thermometers with a red line that rises and falls, traditional in style. Young children who are not yet able to read and understand numbers are still able to understand that the higher the red line, the warmer the temperature. They can visually see that high means hot and low means cold.

Many common household thermometers are made to measure the temperature of the air, indoors or out. Kitchen thermometers often have probes that can be used to measure the temperature of water, meat, or other materials. Young children may associate the words *thermometer* and *temperature* with being ill, because they know that someone takes their temperature when they have a fever. When you introduce different kinds of thermometers to children, be sure to explain and show that many kinds of thermometers are used for different purposes.

Observe and Experiment

Work with children in pairs or small groups. Show them the thermometer and explain how it works. Show them how to safely hold the thermometer and point out how we can "read" the temperature.

Provide an opportunity to show how the temperature changes when there is a contrast between warm and cold. Ask the children, "What do you think is the warmest place in our classroom (or in the school)?" Help children identify a spot near a heating vent or in the sun. Take a temperature reading in that spot. Then ask the children, "What do you think is the coldest place in our school?" If you have access to a refrigerator or freezer, leave the thermometer in that spot for a few minutes, then take a temperature reading. Show the children the contrast: A higher or "bigger" number means that spot is warmer. A lower or "smaller" number means that place is colder.

Document

Take a photo of the thermometer in each of the locations, then print out or project the two images so children can compare how the thermometer looks in the warm spot to how the thermometer looks in the cool spot. Or, if you have two identical or similar thermometers, place them side by side so children can compare.

Reflect

Review what happened in the science experiment by asking children, "Which spot was warmer? Which spot was cooler? How do you know?"

Spark additional conversations and reflection about thermometers and temperature with open-ended questions such as:

- What is a thermometer?
- How does it work?
- Why do people need thermometers?

Think Ahead

The concepts and activities in this chapter connect with children's natural curiosity about the temperature of water, as well as the temperature of other substances such as the air we breathe and the food we eat. The science content knowledge in this chapter and the introduction of the thermometers as a simple tool provide an introduction to the concept of the water cycle that will be presented in chapter 9 and provide a foundation for later science learning.

Chapter Five:

Water and Plants

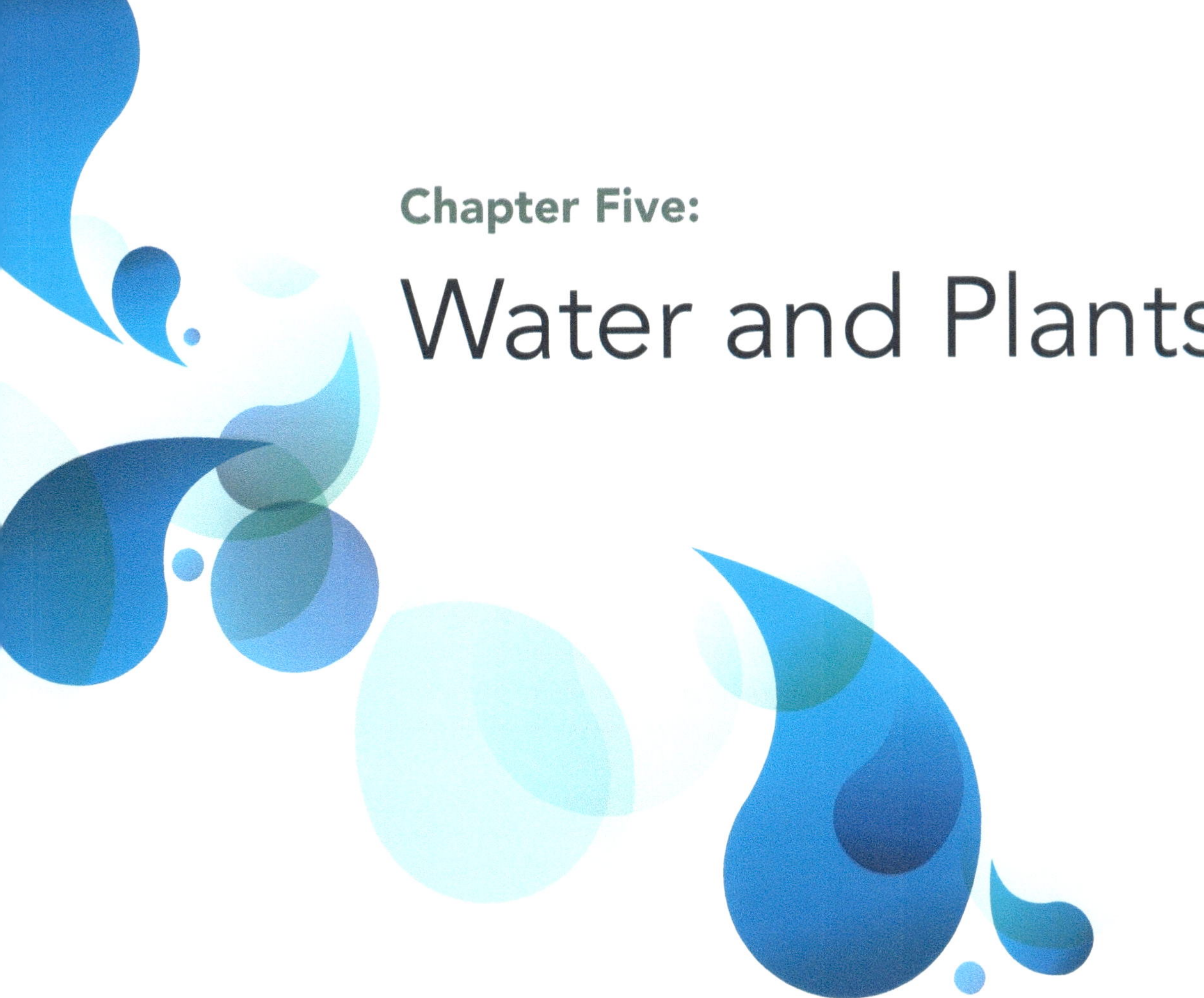

Outside on the playground, teacher Jill fills two child-sized watering cans with water from a spigot while Mia and Teddy, both age four, wait for their turn to water the school garden beds.

Ms. Jill gives them each a full watering can and says, "I'm so happy you're going to help water the garden. The weather has been so hot and dry lately."

Mia and Teddy carry the watering cans over to the raised bed where a group of tomato plants are growing in the sun.

The children begin using the watering cans to sprinkle water on the garden. Mia uses her water to moisten the soil while Teddy uses his water to sprinkle on the leaves of the plants.

Mia says, "Down here, Teddy. Put the water in the dirt."

"No," says Teddy. "The leaves need the water. I'm doing the rain."

Ms. Jill has been standing nearby, observing and listening to the children. "What an interesting conversation!" she says. "It sounds like you both have ideas about where the water should go."

> "Which one is right, Ms. Jill?" asks Mia.
>
> The teacher replies, "That sounds like a question a scientist might ask. I know a science book that might help us learn more about plants."

The experience of planting and caring for a school garden deepens children's understanding of plants and how they grow. As this vignette illustrates, the process also provides many wonderful teachable moments when children can expand their understanding of the relationships between water and plants. The disagreement between Teddy, who wants to water the leaves of the plant, and Mia, who wants to water the soil and roots, provides an opportunity to identify and discuss the parts of plants and their functions. In this chapter, we'll identify some of these key topics that are engaging and developmentally appropriate for young botanists.

Plants Need Water

People and plants have something in common. We all need water to live. The relationship between people and plants, in particular edible plants, is a watery one. Plants give us water and we give plants water. Much of the water human beings take in comes from the plants we eat (UCLA Health, 2022). And some of the water needed by garden plants and farm crops is provided through the effort and ingenuity of people such as farmers and gardeners. In this chapter, we'll explore ways to support children's understanding of the essential role of water in plant life, especially the plants we harvest and eat as food.

Learning Objectives

In the Head Start Early Learning Outcomes Framework, one of the specific examples listed as an indicator that a child is successfully using scientific reasoning is a child's speculation that plants need water to grow. Naming the parts of a plant is included as an example of "observable phenomena."

Head Start Early Learning Outcomes Framework

Goal P-SCI 4. Child asks a question, gathers information, and makes predictions.

Makes predictions and brainstorms solutions based on background knowledge and experiences, such as, "I think that plants need water to grow."

Goal P-SCI 5. Child plans and conducts investigations and experiments.

Implements steps and uses materials to explore testable questions, such as, "Do plants need water to grow?" by planting seeds and giving water to some but not others.

Goal P-SCI 2. Child engages in scientific talk.

Uses scientific content words when investigating and describing observable phenomena, such as parts of a plant, animal, or object (U.S. Department of Health and Human Services, Administration for Children and Families, Office of Head Start, 2015).

Our learning objectives for this chapter are informed by these goals in the Head Start framework, as well as NGSS and NAEYC standards and current research in the field of child development and science education. The four objectives are worded and structured in ways that help you scaffold children's learning experiences, provide meaningful, play-based contexts for learning, and create foundations for future learning.

Chapter 5 Learning Objectives

1. Support children's growing understanding of water as essential to the life of plants.
2. Provide opportunities for children to observe and discuss the role of water in the life cycle of plants.
3. During regular water play and dramatic play indoors and outdoors, expose children to concepts related to water, plants, farming, and food.
4. Conduct teacher-facilitated science activities and experiments that demonstrate the important role of water in the life of plants.

Background Information for Educators

Botany is the branch of biology that focuses on the study of plants. But you don't need a degree in botany to know that plants need water. As a teacher in an early childhood classroom, it is helpful to know how plants take in water and use water to grow.

Water is essential for all plants. Up to 95 percent of a plant's tissue is made of water (Beran, 2023). Water is responsible for many important plant functions, such as the sprouting of seeds as well as photosynthesis. The process of photosynthesis allows plants to use energy from the sun to create their own food. This can't happen without the water that plants absorb from the soil through their roots. Water moves upward through the plant through pipelike vessels called xylem. The roots of a plant play an important role in how plants take in and use water (National Geographic Education, 2025).

Parts of a Plant

Let's briefly review the parts of a plant. Almost all plants have leaves, stems, and roots. Knowing some basic information about these plant parts will help you facilitate observations, explorations, and conversations about plants with young children.

Leaves take in the light that is used to make food for the plant (photosynthesis). Different kinds of plants have different leaves. They have different shapes, sizes, and textures. While leaves do not absorb water like roots, some leaves play a role in directing water to the roots.

Stems connect the roots to the leaves. The stem plays the important role of transporting water from the roots to the leaves and flowers. Stems also support plants and hold the leaves in position where they can take in light. Stems also serve as places of food storage.

Roots absorb nutrients and water from the soil. Roots also provide stability for the plant so it can grow. Different kinds of plants have different kinds of roots. Some plants have a large taproot while others have roots that spread out in many directions. Some roots grow very deep into the soil, and some stay closer to the surface (The Huntington, 2025).

Vocabulary

Irrigation: the watering of land, usually for crops, using artificial structures such as pipes

Leaf: a part of a plant that grows from a stem

Photosynthesis: the process by which a plant makes its own food using energy from light as well as water and air

Root: the part of a plant that grows underground, takes in water from the ground, stores food, and holds the plant in place

Stem: the main trunk of a plant that rises above the soil and supports the leaves and flowers

In early childhood education, we know that relationships are important. The relationship between plants and people is complex. We eat plants. We grow plants. We water plants. Among the first experiences children have caring for another living thing happens when they help water plants in a garden or a pot. Through this simple act, children begin to learn of the many ways people work to grow food and protect the Earth's resources.

Ask a Water Scientist

What are some of the methods farmers use to ensure their crops have the right amount of water?

Irrigation is the method used to provide water for plants used for agriculture. This process can be as simple as using a bucket to water a garden. But commercial farmers use mechanical systems. Some farmers might use large sprinkler systems, and others might use a network of tubing to bring water directly to the roots of the plants. Irrigation systems allow farmers in dry regions to grow crops.

Water used for irrigation might travel a long distance. For example, farmers in Arizona are able to grow crops such as pecans and melons because a series of canals and aqueducts transports water from the Colorado River to these arid regions (USGS, 2018a).

Explore

Think about the children in your classroom and the community in which they live. What plants do they see, use, and eat in their day-to-day lives? Remember that intentional teachers build their curriculum plans and classroom activities around ideas that are relevant and meaningful to the children in their class. When it comes to teaching about plants, that means observing and engaging with plants in the children's direct environment, indoors and out.

Visit Plants in the Children's Environment

To spark interest and inquiry in plants and how they use water, engage children in visiting and observing the plants that grow in and around your school and in and around children's homes.

The types of plants will vary depending on a variety of factors such as the climate and geography in your area, and whether your school is located in an urban, rural, or suburban environment. Even the most developed urban area will still likely have some kinds of plants growing, such as plants in pots on a windowsill or "weeds" growing between cracks in a sidewalk. (By the way, keep in mind that a weed is not the name of a plant. The word *weed* refers to any plant that grows where it is not wanted. For our purposes, as teachers and children searching for plants to observe and study, there are no such things as weeds.)

Similar to the water hunt in chapter 1, take the children on a plant walk outdoors. Or take several plant hunts over a period of time. Plan a walking route that will expose children to a variety of plants such as trees, bushes, grasses, flower beds, and vegetable gardens.

As children discover examples of plants outdoors, ask questions that will prompt them to observe details and consider how the plants receive water, such as, "What do you see?" "What do you notice?" and "I wonder where that plants gets its water." Guide the conversation to help them identify details that demonstrate the differences between plants that receive their water from natural sources of water, such as rain, and water sources that are built by people, such as sprinkler or garden hose.

Document children's discoveries and questions. Take photos and make lists of plants that you see. Give children clipboards with paper and pencils and invite them to sketch the plants they find.

You can conduct similar plant hunts indoors, especially if your school has many potted plants. If possible, take children into the school kitchen and observe where the food is stored. Ask children to identify plants that we eat as food, such as fruits and vegetables.

Visit a Garden or Farm

If possible, take a field trip to a garden or a farm and observe how the crops are watered. Ask a local gardener or farmer to demonstrate how they work to ensure the crops have enough water to grow. Take photos and document children's questions and comments so you can use these later to plan activities that extend learning about plants and water. If you can't, consider visiting a garden virtually. For example, this short video about Brooklyn's Eagle Street Farm shows footage of people tending a rooftop vegetable garden while a narrator explains the value of urban gardening: https://thekidshouldseethis.com/post/8228698185

Tip: When showing online videos to children, be sure to preview and prep the video to avoid ads and links to inappropriate content.

Play

When young children play outdoors where trees and other plants grow, children will often spontaneously incorporate plants into their play. They might run around and hide among trees or bushes. They might use sticks, leaves, and other plants parts as props in their play. An important role of the teacher is to facilitate these open-ended play experiences to ensure that children are safe and that they learn how to treat plants and the natural environment with respect.

Set Clear Expectations that Respect Plants

Often, when a child is interested in a plant, they will want to touch it. Make sure the plants in the children's environment are safe for children to touch. Look for thorns or prickles that might hurt children. Make sure the area is free of poison ivy and other potentially harmful plants.

During play and exploration, children might also want to pick a plant or pull off its leaves or petals. Remember that this desire usually comes from children's curiosity and excitement about plants. Explain to children that a plant is living thing and we must take care not to hurt it. If we pick a plant, it will no longer be able to get water from the soil and it will die. Leaves, petals, or flowers are important parts of a plant, and pulling those off might really hurt the plant and keep it from growing and living. Create clear rules about what children can play with, such as sticks and leaves that have fallen off a plant and are found on the ground.

Exploring Trees

Trees are a special type of plant, due to their size and strength, and children are often interested in exploring and even climbing trees. Teachers can create a safe and engaging outdoor play opportunities centered around tree exploration and climbing by combining careful supervision, clear safety guidelines, and a focus on respect for plants and the natural world. Here's an example of how tree exploration might be facilitated in a preschool setting:

First, check the trees in the area to see if any might be appropriate for touching or climbing. The tree should be inspected for weak branches, sharp surfaces, or anything else that could cause injury.

If the tree has a few low branches that might be strong enough for a young child to climb or sit on, make sure there is a soft landing surface around and under the tree, such as mulch or wood chips. If you are able to identify a tree that might be safe for climbing, set some clear safety expectations for the children. For example, taking turns (one child at a time) and taking care to respect the tree by not pulling off leaves or bark.

Most trees don't naturally grow in positions that allow safe climbing. But there are other ways children can engage with trees during play time. Trees can serve as a shady spot for rest, a "home base" for running games, or serve as a location or character in pretend play.

One sure way to help children learn to respect a tree is to give it a name. Use a field guide, an app, or other reference tool with photos to help children identify the type of tree, such as elm, maple, or oak. A useful resource is the Arbor Day Foundation at https://www.arborday.org/trees/whattree/. Invite children to come up with their own special names for the trees they know and love.

Play Indoors with Natural Materials

Whether or not your outdoor space has many trees or living plants, children can still engage with plants in meaningful ways during indoor play through the use of loose parts that come from plants. (The term *loose parts* refers to open-ended materials that children can move, arrange, sort, and explore in countless ways during play.)

When selecting plant-based loose parts, check items for safety hazards, including sharp edges and potential allergens, such as nuts and seeds. Some examples of loose parts that come from plants include the following:

Pinecones

Acorns

Leaves

Twigs or small branches

Wood slices

Tree bark pieces

Flower petals

Husks from corn or other plants

Cotton pods or fibers

Gourds

Palm fronds

Driftwood

Grass stalks

These items can be used as table toys, added to block constructions, or (my favorite) incorporated into water play in sensory bins and sensory tables. For example, floating leaves or sticks in water and observing how different natural objects interact with water is a great way for children to build understanding through play. Ask open-ended questions and prompt conversations with questions such as, "You put the dry stick in the water. Now it is a wet stick. What do you notice?" Children may make interesting observations about the ways that the color and texture of these materials changes when they get wet. The natural materials can be combined with toy fish or other water-loving animals to enrich pretend play.

Washing and Preparing Food

Another way that plants can be incorporated into play is by inviting children to help wash fruits and vegetables that will be served as a snack. Washing, preparing, and eating plants as snacks is a wonderful way to engage all the children's senses, including sight, sound, touch, smell, and taste.

Here are some examples of fruits and vegetables that are fun for preschool children to wash, prepare, and taste:

Fruits:

- **Apples:** Firm, smooth surface, fun to scrub and rinse
- **Grapes:** Small and round, perfect for rinsing in bunches
- **Strawberries:** Soft texture with tiny seeds on the outside, fun to wash carefully
- **Oranges:** Bumpy skin offers a different texture for scrubbing
- **Pears:** Similar to apples but with a different shape
- **Plums:** Smooth and slippery when wet, fun challenge to handle
- **Bananas (unpeeled):** Washing the outside introduces the concept of washing foods you peel
- **Blueberries:** Tiny and round, fun for rinsing in a small strainer

Vegetables:

- **Carrots:** Long and sometimes a bit dirty, especially if they still have stems
- **Cucumbers:** Smooth and shiny, fun to wash with a brush or sponge
- **Potatoes:** Often very dirty with soil, they require scrubbing
- **Bell peppers:** Smooth and shiny in bright colors, appealing to children
- **Tomatoes:** Soft but smooth, requiring gentle washing
- **Radishes:** Small and round, often with leaves still attached for extra sensory play
- **Zucchini:** Similar to cucumbers but slightly bumpier texture
- **Broccoli:** Interesting texture with many little crevices for a sponge or brush to reach

These fruits and vegetables have a variety of textures, colors, and shapes, making the washing activity more engaging and stimulating for children.

The process of washing fruits or vegetables emphasizes the many important roles of water in our own lives, as a source of nourishment for the plants to grow as well as an essential part of the preparation process. The washing can take place in a clean and sanitized basin of water in the classroom or, if possible, in a sink. The brushes and sponges must also be clean and sanitary, and children must wash hands before they begin.

As children wash the fruits or vegetables, ask questions that encourage them to notice the characteristics of each plant. Ask, "What does this feel like? Is it smooth or bumpy? Is it big or small?" And once each fruit or vegetable is washed, have children place them on a towel to dry. Be sure to follow up the washing activity with an opportunity to taste and share.

Recommended Children's Books

***From Seed to Plant* by Gail Gibbons**

Gail Gibbons is a master of informative, developmentally appropriate nonfiction picture books, and *From Seed to Plant* is one of her best. Simple text and colorful illustrations explain the growth process of a plant.

***How a Seed Grows* by Helene J. Jordan**

There are many children's picture books about seeds and plants, but *How a Seed Grows* is special in its beautiful simplicity. The text and illustrations show several different kinds of seeds and how they grow, such as an acorn that grows into a tall oak tree or a simple bean that grows quickly into a bean plant.

***The City Tree* by Shira Boss**

This book demonstrates that you don't have to live in a rural countryside to know and love plants. The colorful illustrations and story show how caring for a single tree can bring people together and enrich the lives in a community.

***The Curious Garden* by Peter Brown**

The curious gardener in this story is a little boy who creates a beautiful urban paradise along an abandoned elevated railroad track. The story is fanciful but bears some similarity to the real-life High Line in New York City.

***The Carrot Seed* by Ruth Krauss**

The Carrot Seed is such a beloved classic, probably because the main character, a child who plants a seed, is such a fearless optimist. While the speed of growth and the size of the carrot are not exactly scientifically accurate, the book is always a fun read-aloud.

***My Garden* by Kevin Henkes**

Another fanciful take on gardening, this time from the award-winning author–illustrator Kevin Henkes. The story is told by a little girl who imagines, for example, that if she buries a seashell in the ground, it will grow into a seashell plant!

Experiment

Ideally, planting seeds, growing plants, and caring for plants are ongoing activities in any early childhood classroom. These don't have to be short-term science experiments.

Activity: Grow Seeds

Bean plants are easy to germinate from seeds (beans) and they grow quickly, making beans a good choice for classroom gardening. Fava beans, kidney beans, and lima beans are good choices among beans. You can begin by simply germinating the seeds in moist paper towels rather than soil. Clear plastic bags keep the towels moist and allow children to see how the seeds are growing. Some teachers tape the bags to a sunny window, making the germinating seeds even easier to observe.

Prepare

Prepare the materials you will need for germinating seeds, including:

- Dry bean seeds (kidney beans, lima beans, or similar)
- Paper towels
- Plastic sandwich bags (clear, resealable)
- Water spray bottle

Prepare and set aside the materials you will need later for planting the sprouted seeds in soil, such as:

- Small cups or containers (to hold soil)
- Potting soil
- Small spoons or shovels (for soil)
- Labels or stickers (optional, for labeling containers)

Observe and Experiment

Give each child a folded paper towel. Let them gently spray it with water using the spray bottle until it is damp but not soaking wet. Hand out two to three bean seeds to each child. Ask them to place the seeds on one-half of the damp paper towel, then fold the towel over the seeds to cover them. Then help each child put their damp, folded paper towel with the seeds inside into a clear plastic bag. Seal the bag tightly to keep the moisture inside. Label the bags or let the children decorate their bags with stickers. Then place the bags in a sunny spot. Invite the children check on their seeds each day. After a few days, the children will see little roots and shoots starting to grow.

After the seeds have sprouted, it's time to move their sprouts into soil so they can continue to grow. Give each child a small cup or container. Help them fill the container with potting soil using a spoon or small shovel. Help each child open their plastic bag and carefully remove the paper towel with the sprouted seeds. Let them gently place the seed (with its roots) into the soil, root-side down. Then show the children how to gently cover the seed with a small amount of soil, making sure the sprout is sticking out of the top. Next, help the children lightly water the soil, ensuring it's damp but not too wet.

Document

Over the next few weeks, help the children measure and observe how much their plants are growing. You might create a growth chart or charts where the children can record how much their plants have grown over time. Discuss how plants need sunlight, soil, and (of course) water to grow.

Reflect

If any of the plants do not grow, help the children think about why that happened. For example, if one of the bags leaks water and the bean dries up, invite the children to carefully examine the bag, the towel, and the seed. Ask, "What happened here? Why do you think this bean did not grow like the others?"

Impatient? Watch these time-lapse videos:

"Bean Time-Lapse—25 Days I Soil cross section" https://www.youtube.com/watch?v=w77zPAtVTuI

"Growing Pea Time Lapse" https://www.youtube.com/watch?v=jiVIz8R0JWI&t=9s

Activity: Making Juice

Making juice is a fun activity for lots of reasons. Seeing how much juice can come from a piece of fruit or vegetable is a great way to demonstrate to children that a plant's body, like our bodies, is primarily made of water.

Prepare

Many different kinds of fruits and vegetables can be used to make delicious juices. These include oranges, apples, strawberries, carrots, cucumbers, and spinach.

Other materials you'll need include child-safe knives, small cutting boards, and a manual juicer or small blender.

Observe and Experiment

First, wash the fruits and vegetables to make sure they are clean, including rinds and skins that will later be thrown away (see above for washing activity with children). With adult support, children can prepare the fruits or vegetables for juicing by cutting into slices or small pieces. Children can safely cut soft fruits such as bananas or strawberries using plastic safety knives. For harder fruits or vegetables (such as apples or carrots), an adult can cut them into small pieces and the children can help place the pieces in a bowl.

Next, invite children to help place the fruits or vegetables into the blender or juicer. If possible, have the children take turns pressing the start and stop buttons. (Be sure to read and follow all safety instructions for your appliances.) Ideally, position the blender or juicer where children can see how the ingredients move and change as they turn into juice.

Document

If possible, take photos or video of the process. When the juice is ready to taste, note children's comments and observations about the flavor and texture of the juice.

Reflect

If children are able to make and taste different juices, ask children to compare the flavors. Consider creating a bar graph to show which type of juice children like best. For example, create a chart with a picture of each fruit or vegetable at the bottom. Have children place a sticker or a check mark above the one they liked best. Help children place their sticker or mark one above the other, in a line or stack, so you can compare one bar to the other on the graph.

If you have previously introduced children to the word "liquid," ask children to compare the liquid fruit to the solid fruit. Ask children to think, "Where did the liquid come from?" Guide children to understand that fruits and vegetables contain water. The juice is made of both water and other parts of the plant.

Think Ahead

In this chapter, we explored the important relationships between water and plants, as well as the relationships between plants and people. In the next chapter, we'll continue to explore the ways that water is essential to all living things, as we focus on fish and other creatures that live in and around bodies of water.

Chapter Six:

Fish and Other Life in and around Water

"Swimmy, swimmy," says three-year-old Emmie as she holds a small toy fish under the surface of the water. Emmie and several other children in the class are playing in the water in a sensory table. Their teacher, Ms. Jenny, has added toy fish and other toy sea creatures to the water, along with a few cups and spoons.

"Here comes the baby shark," says Tess, playing next to Emmie. "Baby shark wants to swimmy swimmy."

Emmie smiles and moves her toy fish closer to the toy fish that Tess is holding. Tess sings, "Baby, baby, toot toot, baby shark!"

"Swimmy, swimmy, swimmy," says Emmie.

"Let's eat our dinner," says Tess. "Baby shark wants spaghetti."

"Yummy, yummy, yummy," says Emmie.

Ms. Jenny says, "Sounds like the fish are hungry today."

Tess shakes her head. "My fish isn't a fish. It's a shark. A baby shark."

Ms. Jenny replies, "Oh, that's interesting. Your baby shark is not a fish?"

"No," says Tess. "She's too big to be a fish."

"Hmm," says Ms. Jenny. "So a shark is bigger than a fish?"

"Bigger and bigger," Tess nods and turns back to Emmie. "Time to eat your dinner!"

Young children are often fascinated by fish and sea creatures. As demonstrated in the above scenario, their conversations and play are often a mix of facts and fiction about the natural world, likely gleaned from picture books, videos, conversations, and direct experience. Children's curiosity about fish and other animals that live in and around water provides great opportunities to explore the relationships between living creatures and water and how a watery habitat benefits certain kinds of creatures. In this chapter, we'll explore activities and experiences that teach children about the fish and other animals who live in and around the water, in ponds and streams as well as in large bodies of water like the ocean.

Learning Objectives

The teaching and learning about animals that live in and around animals aligns with learning standards related to biology and zoology. The Next Generation Science Standards refer to animals as organisms that live, grow, and have structures.

Next Generation Science Standards

K-LS1-1 Use observations to describe patterns of what plants and animals (including humans) need to survive.

LS1.C Organization for Matter and Energy Flow in Organisms

All animals need food in order to live and grow. They obtain their food from plants or from other animals. Plants need water and light to live and grow (National Research Council, 2013).

The Head Start Early Learning Outcomes Framework also refers to animals as organisms under the domain of Scientific Reasoning and emphasizes the importance of observation.

Head Start Early Learning Outcomes Framework

Goal P-SCI 1. Child observes and describes observable phenomena (objects, materials, organisms, and events).

Goal P-SCI 2. Child engages in scientific talk.

Uses scientific practice words or signs, such as observe, describe, compare, contrast, question, predict, experiment, reflect, cooperate, or measure.

Uses scientific content words when investigating and describing observable phenomena, such as parts of a plant, animal, or object (U.S. Department of Health and Human Services, Administration for Children and Families, Office of Head Start, 2015).

National Association for the Education of Young Children (NAEYC) accreditation standards include the life cycles of organisms as key content.

> **NAEYC Early Learning Program Accreditation Standards and Assessment Items**
>
> **Topic 2.G Science**
>
> Preschoolers and kindergartners should be provided varied experiences and materials to learn key content and principles of science, such as the difference between living and nonliving things (for example, plants versus rocks) (NAEYC, 2022).

Informed by these key documents and frameworks, the following learning objectives can shape our approach to teaching young children about fish and other animals (or organisms) that live in and around water. The four objectives are worded and structured in ways that help you scaffold children's learning experiences, provide meaningful, play-based contexts for learning, and create foundations for future learning.

Chapter 6 Learning Objectives

1. Support children's growing understanding of fish and other animals that live in and around water.
2. Provide opportunities for children to observe and discuss the characteristics, behaviors, and habitats of fish and other animals that live in and around water.
3. During regular water play and dramatic play indoors and outdoors, expose children to concepts related to how different organisms live in habitats that are in or around bodies of water.
4. Conduct teacher-facilitated science activities and experiments that demonstrate the relationship between water and animal life.

Background Information for Educators

There are many different kinds of fish, but all fish share some common essential characteristics. All fish live in water and breathe through gills. Like humans, fish are vertebrates, which means they have backbones. Fish live in both freshwater and saltwater environments (National Geographic Society, 2012). But fish are not the only animals that live in water. There are mammals, such as whales and dolphins, that live in the sea; these are warm-blooded creatures with lungs for breathing. There are water birds, such as pelicans, that live near the water, relying on organisms in the water for their food. And there are amphibians and reptiles, such as frogs and turtles, that live part of their lives in the water and part out of the water (Hurt, 2015).

Vocabulary

Fish: a cold-blooded animal that lives in water, breathes with gills, and usually has fins and scales

Mammal: a warm-blooded animal that feeds milk to its young

Bird: a warm-blooded, feathered animal that has wings

Amphibian: a cold-blooded animal that can live both on land and in water, such as a frog

Reptile: a cold-blooded animal that has a body covered with scales or hard parts, such as a snake or turtle

You've probably heard the expression, "There are plenty of fish in the sea," and this is certainly based on fact. The number of different species of fish is more than twenty-five thousand (Douglas, 2024). Keeping in mind that our focus in this book is water science, it's probably most helpful for us to look at just one distinguishing characteristic: the difference between organisms living in salt water (like oceans) and those living in fresh water (like rivers and lakes). Organisms living in salt water tend to have more protective skin and scales. Freshwater fish and animals tend to be smaller than creatures living in salt water. As you guide children to learn about fish and other animals that live in and around water, it might be helpful to consider the characteristics of the water itself—fresh or salty, as well as warm or cold—characteristics that children can explore through their own senses.

Examples of saltwater fish and animals:

- Clownfish
- Great White Shark
- Sea Turtle
- Dolphin
- Octopus

Examples of freshwater fish and animals:

- Catfish
- Frog
- Otter
- Crayfish
- Piranha

Ask a Water Scientist

Why do some bodies of water have salt water and some have fresh water?

If you've ever had a chance to swim in an ocean, you probably noticed that the water tastes salty. The oceans of the world, such as the Pacific Ocean and the Atlantic Ocean, are really one big salty sea (Duxbury, 2025). Oceans are bodies of salt water. Lakes and rivers, however, are usually fresh water.

When water in the form of rain (or other types of precipitation) falls on Earth, it flows over the land, collecting salts and minerals. It may flow into a river or stream that could take it to a lake. Water usually leaves a lake through an outlet, such as a river, that keeps the water moving and carries away salts and minerals. This movement keeps the water in the lake fresh. When this water, which still has salts and minerals in it, reaches the ocean, the salts and minerals are deposited there as well. Water leaves the ocean through evaporation, which leaves behind the salt, so the ocean remains salty (Petruzzello, 2022). Salt water is not safe for people to drink, but it can be treated to be safe to drink through desalination, a process that removes salts.

Explore

As always, the best way to introduce children to new ideas and concepts is through direct experience. How might you arrange for the children in your class to meet a real fish? Perhaps you already have a pet fish in your classroom or in another area of your school. Perhaps your school is located near a body of water, a park with a koi pond, or even a seafood shop with a lobster tank. Think about what options might be available to provide a direct sensory experience for the children.

If a direct experience is not available, here are some options for short educational videos.

"Why Do Fish School?" https://www.youtube.com/watch?v=XRSS7z6IbL8

"Rare Footage of Ocean Sunfish Getting Cleaned" https://www.youtube.com/watch?v=A1WBilMrDIU

"Curious Lumpsucker, Ponyo Fish, Says Hello" https://www.youtube.com/watch?v=XnmeaS4uiS8

"Underwater Fish Tornado" https://www.youtube.com/watch?v=_Ack-YNt1Zw

"Mein Koi Aussichtsturm im Gartenteich—bei Tag [My Koi Observation Tower in the Garden Pond—during the Day]" https://www.youtube.com/watch?v=mtoonRJdwuc

"Clear Kayaking in the Crystal Clear Water with Manatees." https://www.youtube.com/watch?v=B_1vsCQrXxg

As children observe fish and other water creatures, listen and observe for clues about what children find most fascinating or intriguing.

- Are children noticing the colors and patterns on the bodies of the fish?
- Are they interested in the ways the fish move and swim?
- Are children commenting on the size or shape of the fish?
- Are the children paying attention to the environment or habitat? (To the color of the water, the patterns of light, the plants or stones, the sound or smell in the environment?)

These clues will help you make decisions about what types of play experiences and science experiments you will introduce to children.

Play

Playing with toy fish in water bins and sensory tables, as illustrated in the vignette at the opening of this chapter, is just one way to engage children in hands-on play experiences related to fish and other animals that live in and around water. There will always be some element of make believe in this kind of play, whether or not the fish toys are designed to accurately represent real species of fish. In fact, children often enjoy playing with fish toys and sea creature toys even without any water at all.

Pretend play is an important and valuable experience for children, even without teacher facilitation. Adding some elements of science learning to children's play without interrupting or redirecting children's own ideas takes a light touch. Intentional teachers observe and document children's interests over time and gently introduce materials, questions, and challenges that stimulate children's growing creativity and understanding. For example, suppose several children are playing with a set of toy whales on a blue rug in the classroom. One child comments that she has the "mommy whale" and the other whales are the babies. How might a teacher support this play scenario in ways that make connections to water science content?

If the children seem open to my participation in their play, I might sit with them on the rug and begin a conversation with a comment like, "I see the family of whales swimming together. This blue rug reminds me of water. Are they swimming in the blue water?" If the children want to engage in this kind of conversation, I might ask questions such as, "Where do these whales live? Do they swim in a big ocean? How deep is the water? How cold is the water?" I'd listen to their responses and build on their ideas. If the children decide that the whales live in a cold Arctic ocean, for example, I might suggest that they use blocks to make icebergs. This is just one way teachers can use their own background knowledge of science content to add detail and depth to children's play.

What if your classroom does not have access to any toy fish or toy sea creatures? Children can make their own fish using paper, clay, or recycled materials like cardboard or Styrofoam. Also, children can pretend to be fish! Moving our bodies in ways that look and feel like swimming is fun and good for our bodies and brains. Some children's songs that inspire pretend swimming include "The Goldfish" from the Laurie Berkner Band and "Baby Beluga" by Raffi.

Pretend scuba diving is another fun and fishy activity with preschoolers. Work with children to create a mural showing an underwater ecosystem with water, plants, fish, and water animals, or project a photo or video of an underwater scene on a wall of the classroom. Collect or borrow some swimming masks and flippers that children can wear as props and invite children to pretend they are diving deep into a lake or ocean. Document children's ideas, dialogue, and comments to create a class story about your underwater adventures.

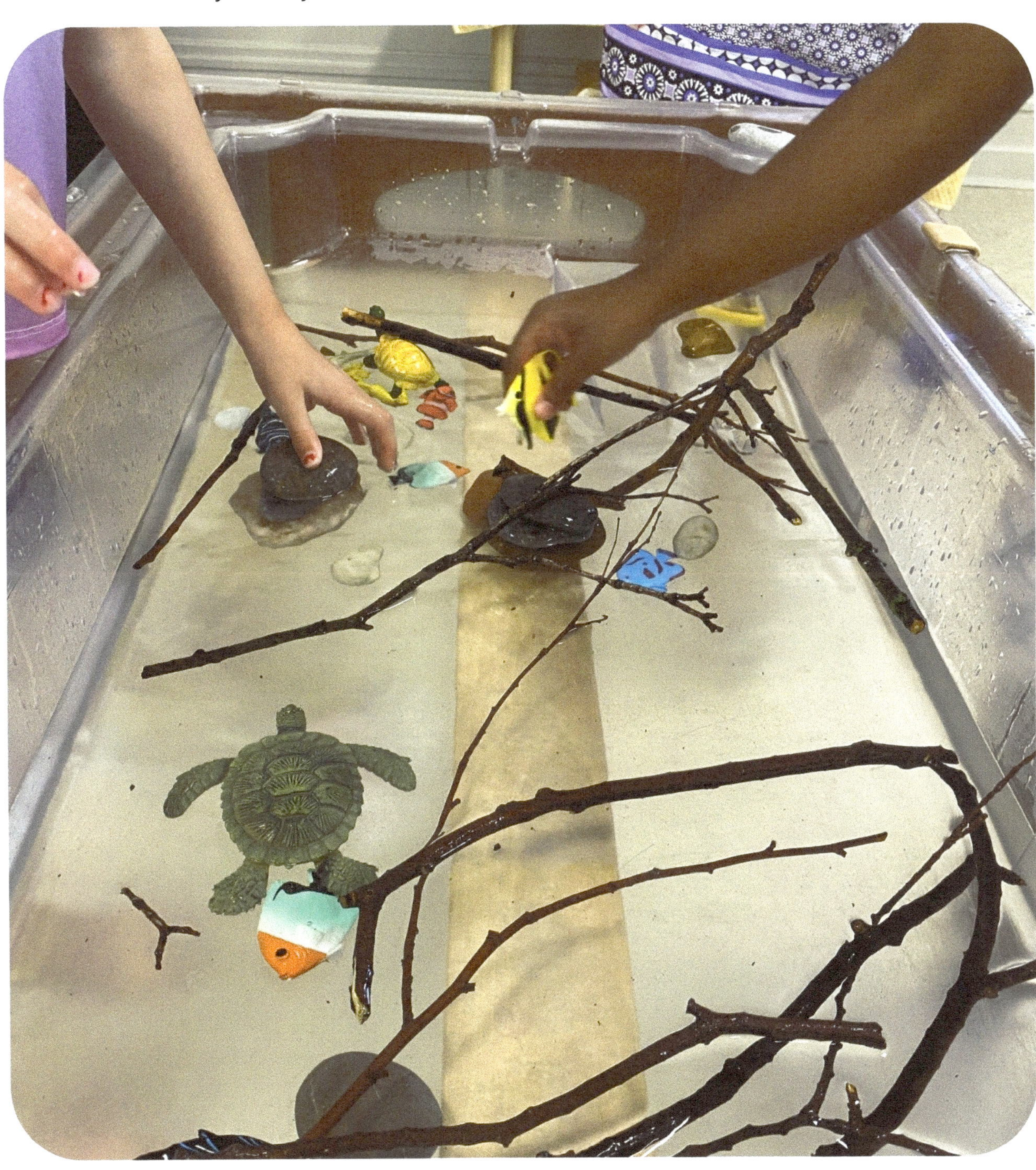

Recommended Children's Books

***Here Comes Ocean* by Meg Fleming**

A child and their dog explore an ocean beach and discover a sand dollar, a sandpiper feather, a small crab, and more.

***Over and Under the Pond* by Kate Messner**

A freshwater ecosystem is described and illustrated in *Over and Under the Pond*. The delight of the book is the interesting contrast between what happens above the surface of the water and what goes on beneath the surface.

***Freaky, Funky Fish: Odd Facts About Fascinating Fish* by Debra Kempf Shumaker**

You might have heard of the electric eel, but did you know there's such a thing as an electric catfish? This nonfiction picture book presents illustrations and facts about a fascinating collection of surprising and unusual fish.

***The Blue Whale* by Jenni Desmond**

This beautiful nonfiction picture book dives into fascinating facts about the largest animal on our planet, the blue whale.

Experiment

Activity: Feed a Fish

Caring for an actual living fish provides direct experience with these fascinating creatures. If your class has access to an aquarium, observing and feeding a fish is a wonderful opportunity to observe their physical characteristics and behaviors.

Prepare

Materials: fish food

The children's role in helping to feed a fish will certainly vary depending on the number and type of fish available, and the methods of feeding. If possible, allow children to see and smell the fish food before it is added to the water. If the fish food is the type that is sprinkled on the surface of the water, children might be able to take turns adding a small amount. Be sure the children wash their hands before and after.

Observe and Experiment

Invite children to closely observe what happens when the food is added. Do the fish respond right away? What do they do? How do they move and swim when there's food in the water? How do they open their mouths? Do they eat quickly or slowly? How do you know?

Document

Invite children to show what they noticed and learned using words (talking, writing, or dictation) or by drawing (on paper with pencils, crayons, or markers) or with their own bodies (by pretending to be fish and acting out what happens when fish are fed).

Reflect

Challenge children to consider: How are fish mealtimes the same or different from people mealtimes?

Activity: Compare Fresh Water to Salt Water

In communities located near a coastline, many children grow up knowing the salty taste of the sea. If the children in your class are curious about the differences between the fresh water of lakes and rivers and the salt water of the seas and oceans, conduct a taste test that provides a sensory demonstration.

Prepare

Materials: cups, a pitcher of drinking water, table salt (ideally in a saltshaker so only a little comes out at a time)

For this activity, do not use water taken directly from bodies of water. Use safe drinking water from the tap or bottled water.

Observe and Experiment

Give each child a cup of fresh drinking water and invite them to take a drink. Ask each child to describe how the water tastes. Often children will say that water tastes like "nothing" because the taste of water is so familiar. Prompt children to slow down and really notice the taste and feel of the fresh water on their tongue.

Next, allow children to add a small amount of salt to their cup of water. (Use a saltshaker with small holes that will only allow a small amount of salt to come out.) Then, invite children to taste the water again. Ask, "What does the salty water taste like?" Most children will not like the taste!

Reflect

Explain or remind children that the water found in seas and oceans is naturally salty. We don't like to drink salt water, but many kinds of fish and sea creatures need to swim in salt water to live. Show the children some photos of saltwater fish and animals from nonfiction reference books or websites such as the *National Geographic Kids Ultimate Oceanpedia* (Wilsdon, 2016). Invite children to draw their own pictures of saltwater organisms, real or imagined.

Think Ahead

Both children and adults often enjoy stories and activities involving fish and other creatures that live in watery habitats. I think there's something about the beauty of bodies of water, such as great lakes and vast oceans, as well as the graceful movements of water-borne creatures, that draws us in and inspires us to learn more. In our next chapter, we'll move from what happens underwater to what happens above the water, as we explore how and why things float.

Chapter Seven:

Boats and Other Things that Float

During free-play time, a small group of preschool children are playing with toy boats and water in a sensory table. The boats are small plastic toys that easily float on the surface of the water. (The toys are hollow, allowing space for a pocket of air inside.)

One child, Remy, also uses a plastic cup to scoop up and pour water.

"A storm is coming! Here comes a tidal wave!" says Remy as he pours water on his boat.

"Try it, Fiona," says Remy, handing his friend the cup.

Fiona shakes her head. "I don't want to sink it."

Remy says, "It won't sink. The boats are too strong." Remy pours a full cup of water directly onto his boat. The boat tips over but then pops back to the surface.

Fiona watches, then takes the cup and pours water onto her boat, which also tips over but pops back to the surface.

"See?" says Remy. "Our boats are strong!"

Teacher Mary is standing nearby, observing the children. She muses, "I see that your boats didn't sink. I wonder why."

Fiona replies, "Because they're strong!"

Mary asks, "What makes them so strong?"

Remy says, "I don't know."

Mary says, "Maybe we could figure this out together."

In this scenario, the teacher has discovered a moment during ordinary play that could become a gateway to exciting science learning. The children have discovered by observing and testing that the toy boats do not sink. Mary notices the children are using the word *strong* to describe the boats and asks the children an open-ended question to check their understanding. This conversation could lead to several kinds of follow-up activities in which the teacher scaffolds their learning about why some things float.

It seems like just about every curriculum book written for preschool and kindergarten teachers includes some kind of "sink or float" activity. Usually, children are given a combination of objects made of different materials and invited to test them in water to see if they will sink or float. This can be a very fun activity, but what comes next? Once children become skilled at predicting if something will sink or float, the next step is to ask, "Why?" Invite children to wonder and explore: Why do some things sink and others float? And why does it matter?

The content of this chapter goes beyond the classic "Sink or Float?" sorting activities and dives deep into the important question of "Why?" Activities and resources provide guidance on developmentally appropriate ways to teach about *buoyancy* and *density*.

Learning Objectives

Scientific reasoning, according to the Head Start Early Learning Outcomes Framework, includes the comparing and categorizing of "observable phenomena." In a preschool and kindergarten classroom, concepts such as buoyancy and density are certainly "observable phenomena."

Head Start Early Learning Outcomes Framework

Goal P-SCI 3. Child compares and categorizes observable phenomena.

Categorizes by sorting observable phenomena into groups based on attributes such as appearance, weight, function, ability, texture, odor, and sound (U.S. Department of Health and Human Services, Administration for Children and Families, Office of Head Start, 2015).

Additionally, the Head Start framework acknowledges the significance of making predictions and comparing the actual outcomes to the prediction, an experience that happens frequently when children experiment with sinking and floating.

Goal P-SCI 6. Child analyzes results, draws conclusions, and communicates results.

With adult support, compares results to initial prediction and offers evidence as to why they do or do not work. Generates new testable questions based on results (U.S. Department of Health and Human Services, Administration for Children and Families, Office of Head Start, 2015).

Informed by resources such as the Head Start Framework, NAEYC accreditation standards, and NGSS practices, the following learning objectives are developmentally informed and responsive. The three objectives are worded and structured in ways that help you scaffold children's learning experiences, provide meaningful, play-based contexts for learning, and create foundations for future learning.

Chapter 7 Learning Objectives

1. Support children's growing understanding of buoyancy, density, and why some objects sink and others float.
2. During regular water play indoors and outdoors, invite children to experiment and play with a variety of items and materials to observe and test which items float and which sink.
3. Conduct teacher-facilitated science activities and experiments that demonstrate the concepts of buoyance and density.

Background Information for Educators

The first time I prepared to introduce young children to the terms *buoyancy* and *density*, I wasn't sure if they would be interested and responsive to these vocabulary terms and concepts. But I was curious about how they would respond and decided to include these terms in a group discussion at circle time.

As we sat together on the rug, I held up a toy boat and asked, "What do you think will happen if I put this toy in the water table?" One child responded, "It will float!"

Then I asked my favorite question, "Why?" I paused and waited a moment, giving the children time to think. "Why does the boat float?"

To my surprise, one of the children replied, "Buoyancy!" I was excited that one of the children already knew this word and I asked her how she knew. She explained that the word was part of a *Curious George* video she had seen.

Sure enough, the PBS Kids animated series *Curious George* includes a segment called "How Do Boats Float?" (see https://www.youtube.com/watch?v=VnLccU8mihQ) that offers an explanation of both density and buoyancy.

As the PBS Kids video describes, weight is not what determines if something sinks or floats. It is density that matters. *Density* is the amount of something packed into in a particular space. For example, a dry sponge is light because it is not very dense. A rock, however, is denser than a sponge. *Density* refers to both how much something weighs and how much space it takes up. *Buoyancy*, then, is the term that describes why things float or sink and takes into account concepts like *density* as well as forces like gravity.

While I sometimes recommend using short videos to demonstrate science concepts to young children, I usually wait until after the children have had time for some hands-on play and exploration first, before showing a video. In this case, I was surprised and impressed that one of the children remembered information from a video she had viewed at home. The lesson to me, as an intentional teacher, is that I sometimes underestimate children's prior knowledge about science concepts.

Ask a Water Scientist

How does something as heavy as a cruise ship stay afloat? Buoyancy! Buoyancy is the force that allows water to push up against the weight of an object (such as boat). At the same time, the weight of that object is pushing down onto the surface of the water. An object will float if its weight is less than the buoyant force.

Let's dig a little deeper. Buoyancy is related to density. Density is a measurement that shows how tightly or loosely a material is distributed in that space. When an object is less dense than the water it displaces, it will float. For example, imagine a small maple leaf that falls on the surface of a pond. The leaf is less dense than the water, so it floats. When an object is more dense than water, such as a rock, it will sink.

An object can be very large and still float. For example, a cruise ship can weigh more than 200,000 tons, but it is still less dense than the water it displaces because of the air in the hollow hull of the ship. A huge cruise ship will float in water, but a small rock that is more dense than the water it displaces will sink (Stewart, 2023).

The Story of Archimedes

A discussion of buoyancy is not complete without a mention of the Greek mathematician Archimedes. An ancient story describes how Archimedes discovered the concept of buoyancy while he was taking a bath. He noticed that objects in water displace (or move out of the way) some of the water. He figured out that the weight of the water displaced by a floating object must be greater than the object itself. Archimedes' principle, also known as the physical law of buoyancy, states that any object completely or partially submerged in a liquid is acted upon by an upward buoyant force. The magnitude of that force is equal to the weight of the fluid displaced by the body. Today, the concepts of force, gravity, and density as illustrated by Archimedes' principle give us a full understanding of buoyancy.

Vocabulary

Float: to rest on the surface of a liquid such as water

Sink: to drop or fall below the surface

Buoyancy: the tendency of an object to float in a liquid

Density: a measurement that shows how tightly or loosely a material is distributed in a space

Explore

As stated throughout this book, the best way to introduce and spark interest in a science topic is through children's direct experience in their daily lives. What is the child's most direct engagement with concepts of buoyancy and density? Like Archimedes, children's most meaningful experiences with sinking and floating probably happen when they are taking a bath or swimming. During these experiences, the child is literally immersed in water science!

Partner with Families

Bathing or swimming at school is not a common experience in most early childhood programs. In most circumstances, the way to connect science concepts at school with bathing and swimming experiences is through partnerships with parents and caregivers. Invite families to help document children's experiences with floating and sinking at home. Parents and caregivers can ask their child, "When you take a bath, what floats and what sinks?" Ask families to write down their ideas and observations. Then create a two-column chart at school that shows the responses from families.

Under "What floats?" families may report with answers such as, "a bar of soap" or "a bath toy."

Under "What sinks?" a child may report answers such as, "the plug for the drain" or "me!"

Another way to partner with families is to give each family a toy rubber duck to take home and test in the bathtub or sink. Invite families to report back whether the toy sinks or floats, as well as other details about the duck's experience in water at home.

Speaking of rubber ducks, did you know that in 1992 there was a shipping incident in which thousands of ducks and other bath toys were accidently dumped into the Pacific Ocean? This true story is the inspiration for several picture books. Eric Carle's 2005 picture book *10 Little Rubber Ducks* is a whimsical take on the adventures of the stray ducks. *Ducks Overboard!: A True Story of Plastic in Our Oceans* by Markus Motum published in 2021 acknowledges the environmental impact of toys and other items that get lost in the ocean. (Adults can learn more about this true story by reading *Moby-Duck: The True Story of 28,800 Bath Toys Lost at Sea* by Donovan Hohn.) These picture books can be an engaging addition to discussions of sinking and floating, as well as activities related to caring for our oceans as covered in chapters 10 and 11.

Visit, Observe, or Ride in a Real Boat

Is your school community located near a body of water? Are any of the parents and family members in your program involved in shipping, fishing, or transportation industries? A field trip to see a real boat is a fantastic opportunity to make science concepts related to buoyancy come alive.

If a visit to a real boat is not available to you, here are a few educational videos that will spark interest and inspire play and discussion.

"Travel from Rotterdam to Amsterdam in 10 Minutes by Boat: A 4k Timelapse"
https://www.youtube.com/watch?v=HfPCdJapIXA&t=1s

"Over 600 Ships Arriving at the Port of Amsterdam" https://thekidshouldseethis.com/post/over-600-ships-arriving-at-the-port-of-amsterdam-sail-2015

"The Construction of 300 Metre AIDAprima Cruise Ship Cinematic Time Lapse" https://www.youtube.com/watch?v=lavm7CausyA

"Breaking Ice on the Hudson River" https://www.youtube.com/watch?v=mrVM-jMIHLI

Play

Every time children engage in water play, they are exposed to concepts of buoyance and density. All the play activities described in this book will expand and deepen children's experience with these concepts. However, educators can make intentional experiences about the kinds of materials that are presented for play, and the questions asked during play, that will heighten children's awareness of and understanding of what sinks and what floats.

Here are some suggestions of materials that provide excellent opportunities to explore buoyancy and density through hands-on play.

- **Plastic toys:** Lightweight toys such as rubber ducks, plastic boats, or toy animals that float on water can be fun for children to engage with.
- **Sponges:** Sponges are especially interesting because they float at first, but when they soak up water, they sink. Children can see and feel how the sponge changes as it gets heavier.
- **Foam blocks:** Foam floats easily and is soft to handle, making it an ideal material for water play that demonstrates buoyancy.
- **Rocks:** Smooth pebbles or small rocks sink, which provides opportunities for children to compare them with floating objects.
- **Wooden blocks, craft sticks, or other wood objects:** Most wood floats, so using wooden pieces is another way to explore buoyancy. Keep in mind that water can warp or discolor wooden blocks, so I suggest using only old, discarded blocks for water play.
- **Leaves and other natural materials found outdoors:** Adding leaves to water shows how some natural objects easily float on the surface.

As children play with different materials in water, ask open-ended questions that draw children's attention to the properties of the materials that help them float or sink. Questions might include the following:

- What do you think will happen when you add this to the water?
- I wonder why this thing floats but that one does not. Do you have any ideas about that?
- What could be done to make this float?
- What could we do to make this sink?
- These two things are both floating. What do they have in common? How are they the same?

- What do you notice when you push that under the water? What happens?
- What do you think would happen if we added more water? Would that change how things float?

As always, encourage children to explain their thinking with prompts like, "Hmm, tell me more about that," or "That's so interesting. Why do you think that's true?"

Build Boats

Invite children to build their own boats and test how they float in the water bins or sensory tables. Present a selection of materials and allow children to create their own designs.

For example, materials that might make a buoyant base of a boat include:

- Styrofoam pieces
- Sponges
- Aluminum foil
- Small plastic items such as yogurt tubs, condiment containers, and jar lids

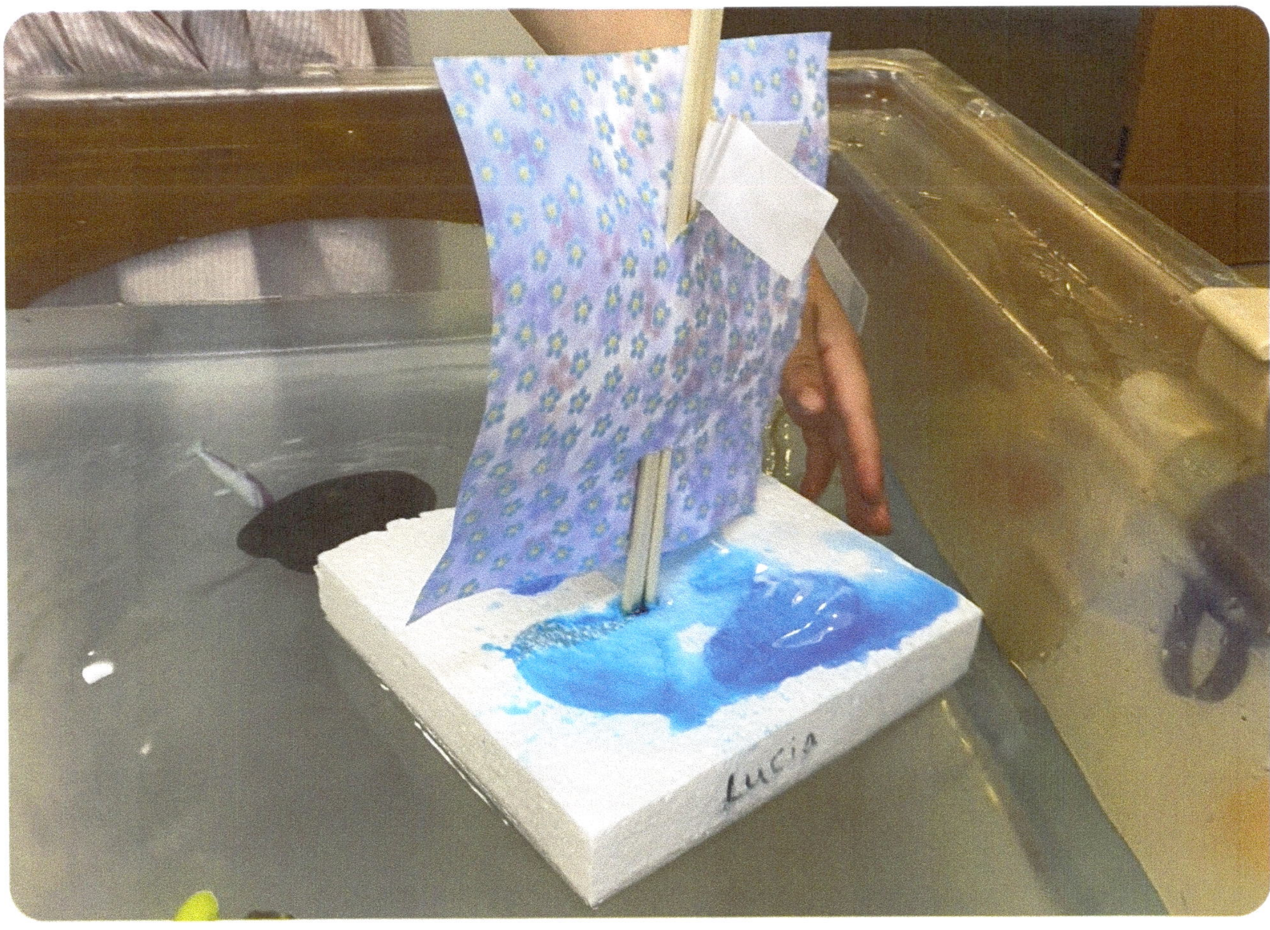

Provide toothpicks or chopsticks to make flags or masts, paper for sails, and tape to hold things together. Allow children the opportunity to experiment with different designs and materials even if you can see that their boat is not seaworthy. Testing their designs and figuring out solutions is an important part of the learning process. Of course, some children are less able to tolerate frustration than others and will need support and direction from teachers. Often, a few helpful suggestions are enough to keep children engaged and practicing creative problem-solving.

Recommended Children's Books

***Who Sank the Boat?* by Pamela Allen**

***Mr. Gumpy's Outing* by John Burningham**

These two classic picture books are remarkably similar in plot. In each story, a varied group of friends go for a boat ride, with mixed results. Children will enjoy comparing the two books and discussing how the disasters could have been averted.

Experiment

Activity: Sink or Float Challenge

Most children are quick to understand that a rubber duck will float and a rock will sink. In this science experiment, present children with a unique challenge: Can you make the duck sink? And can you make the rock float?

Prepare

Materials: bins or sensory table for holding water, 3–4 rubber ducks, and 3–4 rocks or stones (about the same size as the ducks)

Each child will need access to water—a sensory table or bins filled with water at least 3 inches deep. This experiment works best when each child has their own duck and rock to work with and the children are working side by side. Small groups of three or four children are probably ideal.

Observe and Experiment

Allow children to try to manipulate the duck and stone in the water and observe what they do. Children will likely try to hold the duck under water and use their hands or the rock to make it stay. Some children may quickly discover that if they squeeze all the air out of the duck and fill it with water, the duck will sink (Archimedes' Principle!). Some children may try to work together to stack their rocks to keep one of the rocks "floating" above the water.

Some children may request additional materials to make the stone float. Decide in advance which materials you might want to make available. Some of the boat-making materials mentioned previously might be used to construct a floating platform for the rock.

Document

Take photos or video of the children's efforts to accomplish this challenge. Note their predictions and observations.

Reflect

Review together what happened. What did they try? What worked? What didn't work? And why?

Activity: Test the Strength of a Paper Boat

Daniel Miyares's wordless picture book *Float* makes a great introduction to this science experiment. In the book, a child dressed in rain gear launches a little paper boat that travels through puddles and then through gutters, drains, and beyond.

Prepare

Materials: paper (not too thick), a collection of small items such as coins, trays or bins to hold water (or sensory table) filled with just an inch or two of water

Create a flotilla of paper boats similar to the paper boat in the picture book. I like to create two per child: one to use for the experiment and one to color and take home. Some older children may be able to help fold the boats, but this can be tricky! If you need instructions on how to create simple paper boats, a quick search online will provide you with lots of resources (see, for example, https://www.wikihow.com/Make-a-Paper-Boat).

Collect small items that can be placed inside the folds of the boats to test its strength. Examples include coins (I like to use nickels), marbles, or buttons.

Observe and Experiment

Present the children with the paper boats and offer them a challenge. How strong is a paper boat? How can we measure its strength? Guide children to understand that we can test the boats' strength by checking whether they can carry something heavy.

Show children how to place the boat in the water (at the sensory table or in bins) and carefully add a few small items to the boat. The children will discover that a paper boat can't hold much weight—usually just a few nickels or marbles before it begins to tip, tear, and sink.

Document

Take photos or video of the children's efforts to accomplish this challenge. Note their predictions and observations.

Reflect

Review together what happened. How strong were the paper boats? How do you know? Then go back to the picture book *Float* and ask children to compare their own experience with the experience of the boy in the story.

Remember that learning about what sinks and what floats is something that will happen anytime children engage in water play. The information and activities presented in this chapter can be used in combination with other ideas in this book.

Think Ahead

In this chapter, we explored how and why different objects float in water, with a focus on boats. As you explore these concepts and activities with young children, they may talk about other ideas for getting across a body of water, such as bridges and tunnels. In the next chapter, we'll focus on conversations and activities that explore these kinds of human-made structures, also known as the "built environment."

SUPERSTRUCTURES
Bridges
Bridges

Chapter Eight:

Water and the Built Environment

Four-year-olds Mimi and Lian are playing together in the block area of their preschool classroom. Mimi is building one structure with unit blocks, and Lian, at her side, is building another one.

"I'm making a house for a mermaid," says Mimi.

"Me too," says Lian. "I'm making a mermaid house too."

They each stack blocks and create square structures with towers.

Mimi says, "My mermaid likes seaweed. I'm going to add some seaweed." Mimi takes some green paper scraps from the art bin and tears the paper into small pieces. She sprinkles pieces of green paper on the top of her house.

Lian says, "My mermaid likes seaweed too. Can I have some?"

"Here," says Mimi, handing Lian the paper. "You have to tear it up." The girls continue tearing up the green paper and sprinkling it around their houses.

Their teacher, Ms. Kirsten, watches from the art table. Mimi says, "Look, Ms. Kirsten. We're making mermaid houses."

"I see," says Ms. Kirsten. "I've been watching you build. You both have been working hard for a long time."

Lian says, "Let's put our houses together. They can be connected."

Mimi says, "No, I don't want the houses together."

Lian starts adding blocks to the space between the two houses.

"No," says Mimi. "Stop!"

Ms. Kirsten walks over to the block area. "I heard Mimi say 'stop.'"

Lian sits down on the rug and hides her face in her hands. Ms. Kirsten says, gently, "Lian, tell Mimi your idea. What did you want to do?"

Lian picks up a block and holds it in the space between the two mermaid houses. "This," she says.

Ms. Kirsten says, "You want to put a block between the two houses. That looks like a bridge."

Lian smiles and nods.

Ms. Kirsten says, "Ask Mimi. Ask if you can build a bridge between the two houses."

Lian turns to Mimi and says, "Can we build a bridge?"

Mimi nods. "Okay, we can make an ocean bridge for the mermaids."

In this vignette, two preschool children are playing with blocks. There's no water involved in their play, and yet the children are imagining water as they build houses for mermaids. While it's not clear if these imaginary mermaid houses are underwater or next to the water, the children have incorporated science concepts into their play. They've demonstrated an understanding that "seaweed" is a plant that is green and grows in the water. And they have experimented with creating a *built environment* that includes an "ocean bridge."

Engineers use the term "built environment" to refer to structures that are made by humans, such as houses, buildings, roads, and bridges. There is a particular category of structures in the built environment that is especially relevant to water: large structures such as bridges, dams, canals, and tunnels, as well as smaller, everyday structures such as gutters, storm drains, and hoses. In this chapter, we'll focus on preschool and kindergarten activities that involve construction play, and we'll explore the ways that we can combine the fun and excitement of construction play with concepts of water science and civil engineering. The focus of this chapter and the next is how people live with water—the ways we humans travel over, under, and around bodies of water, and the ways we manage water in our environment.

Learning Objectives

In our previous chapters, we focused on water science concepts that are primarily related to Earth science, environmental science, and biology. In this chapter, we focus on the construction play as it is connected to civil engineering and the built environment. Construction play is especially rich in learning opportunities because it can inspire and support exploration of mathematical concepts.

When children play with construction toys that are organized in mathematical systems, such as unit blocks, DUPLO bricks, and LEGO bricks, they are engaged in activities that use nonstandard units of measurement. Every unit block is 5 ½ inches long. While the supplemental pieces vary in size, every basic DUPLO brick is 16 millimeters long. Every basic LEGO brick is 8 millimeters long. The uniformity of these measurements and the relationships between the standard bricks with the rest of pieces in that same system means that construction play has all kinds of mathematical concepts baked into the play experiences. Two half-unit blocks equal one unit, for example. The child doesn't need to know fractions to experience that beautiful ratio as they build.

Let's look at how construction play is aligned with national standards for early learning in the Head Start Early Learning Outcomes Framework, NAEYC accreditation standards, and Next Generation Science Standards.

Head Start Early Learning Outcomes Framework

Domain: Mathematics Development

Goal P-MATH 4. Child compares numbers.

Begins to accurately count and compare objects that are about the same size and are in small groups with adult assistance, such as counts a pile of 2 blocks and a pile of 4, and determines whether the piles have the same or different numbers of blocks.

Domain: Scientific Reasoning

Goal P-SCI 3. Child compares and categorizes observable phenomena.

Uses measurement tools, such as... unit blocks (U.S. Department of Health and Human Services, Administration for Children and Families, Office of Head Start, 2015).

NAEYC Early Learning Program Accreditation Standards and Assessment Items

Topic 2.F Early Mathematics

Offers ideas to support children in beginning to learn math concepts such as numbers, operations, attributes, geometry, measurement, time, patterns, and vocabulary (NAEYC, 2022).

Next Generation Science Standards

Engineering, Technology, and Applications of Science

ETS1.A Defining Engineering Problems

A situation that people want to change or create can be approached as a problem to be solved through engineering. Such problems may have many acceptable solutions.

ETS1.A Defining and Delimiting an Engineering Problem

Asking questions, making observations, and gathering information are helpful in thinking about problems (National Research Council, 2013).

Informed by these frameworks, the chapter objectives are worded and structured in ways that help you scaffold children's learning experiences, provide meaningful, play-based contexts for learning, and create foundations for future learning.

Chapter 8 Learning Objectives

1. Support children's growing understanding of the ways people build structures to manage water and live with water.
2. Provide opportunities for children to observe and discuss the built environment in relation to water, such as bridges, dams, canals, and tunnels.
3. During regular water play and construction play, indoors and outdoors, expose children to play experiences and challenges that allow children to explore and discover how to build structures like bridges, dams, canals, and tunnels.
4. Conduct teacher-facilitated science activities and experiments that demonstrate and test different construction techniques.

Background Information for Educators

Civil engineering is the branch of engineering concerned with designing, building, and maintaining the foundation for our modern society (American Society of Civil Engineers, 2024). Bridges, tunnels, dams, and canals are all examples of civil engineering projects that are in some way related to water. A bridge allows for transportation over water. A tunnel allows transportation under or through water. A dam holds back water, and a canal diverts water.

Vocabulary

Bridge: a structure built over an obstacle (such as a river) that allows travel across

Canal: a long, narrow channel that is filled with water, created for transportation or irrigation

Tunnel: a passageway that goes through or under an obstruction such as a hill

Dam: a structure built to stop water, ice, or soil from flowing

Ask a Water Scientist

What kinds of structures help prevent flooding? For thousands of years, people have been building structures that control water. Among the most famous examples are the walls of earth called dikes built in the Netherlands to prevent flooding (Asterra, 2022). Dams and levees are other examples of structures used to prevent flooding. Like dikes, dams are barriers built across running water to hold it back. Dams can be quite large, such as the massive Hoover Dam built on the Colorado River. Levees are ridges that are built parallel to running water and provide a barrier in the case of flooding. For example, the Mississippi River and Tributaries levee system consists of 2,203 miles of levees that run along the Mississippi, Arkansas, and Red Rivers. This levee systems creates a physical barrier that prevents flooding and protects communities along the riverways (National Geographic Society, 2024).

Mathematical Concepts Related to Construction

The activities in this chapter use the built environment and water as inspiration for construction play using blocks, bricks, and other construction materials. This kind of construction play creates opportunities for children to explore mathematical concepts of shape, measurement, and spatial relationships. According to the Erikson Institute Early Math Collaborative (2014), these concepts are among the "big ideas" of early math children need to explore between the ages of three and six.

- **Shape:** Construction play with blocks involves manipulating three-dimensional solids such as cubes, cylinders, and triangular prisms.
- **Measurement:** Measurement is a mathematical procedure children apply to construction play as they align blocks or other materials to create structures or sequences.
- **Spatial Relationships:** Children develop understanding of spatial relationships as they make connections between physical objects (such as blocks) and their positions or arrangement in space.

As educators, knowing that these are important mathematical concepts helps us to be more intentional and observant in the ways we plan and engage in classroom activities.

Explore

Is your school community located near a bridge, a dam, a tunnel, or a canal? A field trip or walking trip to see one of these structures is a fantastic opportunity to make engineering concepts related to water come alive. For example, if there is a bridge in your neighborhood that you can safely observe on a walk, invite children to consider some of the following questions:

- "What materials do you think were used to build this bridge? How do you know?"
- "What do you think was here in this spot before there was a bridge?"

- "Why do you think a bridge was needed in this spot?"
- If the bridge spans a body of water such as a river, ask children, "Before they had a bridge, how do you think people got across the river?"
- "Who uses this bridge? How do you know?"

If a visit to a structure is not available to you, here are a few educational videos that will spark interest and inspire play and discussion.

"The Brilliant Engineering and Beauty of the Llangollen Canal"
https://www.youtube.com/watch?v=l3ZDFxhY7aQ&t=4s

"Building 10 Movable LEGO Bridges"
https://www.youtube.com/watch?v=u6wC_4ah4fA

"M-O-D-U-S in V-E-N-I-C-E"
https://www.youtube.com/watch?v=lFRnb86IsHI&t=1s

"Brooklyn Bridge New York"
https://www.youtube.com/watch?v=a2ZF--AUeW8

Play

No matter what kinds of structures children are building, construction play with blocks or other materials is a beneficial experience supporting all domains of development—cognitive, physical, and social. As mentioned earlier in this chapter, when children play with toys that are designed to fit together as a system, like wooden unit blocks or plastic bricks or magnetic tiles, the free exploration of these materials during play gives children a sensory and kinesthetic experience with mathematical concepts related to shape, ratios, measurement, and even fractions.

Educators inspired by the Reggio Emilia approach use the term *provocation* to refer to invitations to play that teachers create to provoke learning and engagement. I think of water as a grand provocation for construction play. The presence of water—real, imagined, or represented—is a design challenge. In the block corner, children are invited to think like civil engineers and create structures that incorporate or accommodate water by building over it, under it, or around it. In my experience in preschool classrooms, the most interesting and accessible civil engineering project is the bridge.

Use blue fabric or blue paper to represent water during construction play. Place a strip of blue fabric across the floor of the block corner and let the children decide what happens next. Or add a few small dolls and invite the children to solve a problem: "These little people need to travel to the other side of the river. How will they get across the river?" Another prompt that might inspire bridge building is placing some photos of interesting bridges in the play area or setting aside some picture books about bridges as reference tools.

You can use real water as a provocation for construction play when blocks are used in a sensory bin or table. Plastic bricks or foam shapes are usually waterproof and will not be damaged by water. Outdoors, construction play with real water can take place in areas of sand or mud. After a rain, children enjoy using natural materials like sticks and leaves to build both dams and bridges.

Recommended Children's Books

***Bridges* by Marc Majewski**

It's easy to find photographs of landmark bridges around the world in reference books and online, but Marc Majewski's colorful illustrations and child-friendly text takes us to famous bridges across the globe, including the Golden Gate Bridge, Tower Bridge, and Victoria Falls Bridge.

***The Cow Who Fell in the Canal* by Phyllis Krasilovsky**

Henrika the Dutch cow is the main character in this classic picture book originally published in the 1950s. Peter Spiers's charming illustrations also provide a visual introduction to the Dutch canal system.

***A River* by Marc Martin**

The illustrations in Marc Martin's dreamy wordless picture book follow the varied path of an imaginary river can serve as an inspiration for conversation and construction play.

***Iggy Peck, Architect* by Andrea Beaty**

This first book in Beaty's popular Questioneers series is notable because the protagonist, Iggy, saves the day by building a bridge out of found materials. If the children in your class enjoy this book, try presenting them with a jumble of found materials (such as cardboard tubes and craft chenille sticks) and challenge them to collaborate to construct a bridge!

Experiment

Activity: Build and Test a Bridge

The picture book *Twenty-One Elephants and Still Standing* by April Jones Prince tells the true story of the opening of the Brooklyn Bridge in 1883. The circus showman P.T. Barnum arranged to have twenty-one circus elephants parade across the bridge to demonstrate the strength of the structure (and seize some great publicity for his circus). This picture book also provides a great provocation for inviting children to both build bridges and test their strength.

Prepare

Materials: blocks, toy elephants or other toy animals

Read aloud the book *Twenty-One Elephants and Still Standing* and discuss. Ask open-ended questions such as:

- Why were some people afraid to cross the Brooklyn Bridge?
- Why did the elephants parade across the bridge?
- What happened?
- Did the elephants change how people thought about the bridge?

Observe and Experiment

Invite children to build and test their own bridges using the materials available in your classroom. Children may enjoy using toy elephants or other animal toys to test the strength of their bridges. Durable construction toys like wooden blocks and plastic bricks are quite strong and, if children are skilled at building stable and balanced structures, will hold quite a lot of animals. As an added challenge, invite children to use materials like cardboard, egg cartons, or craft sticks to build their structures.

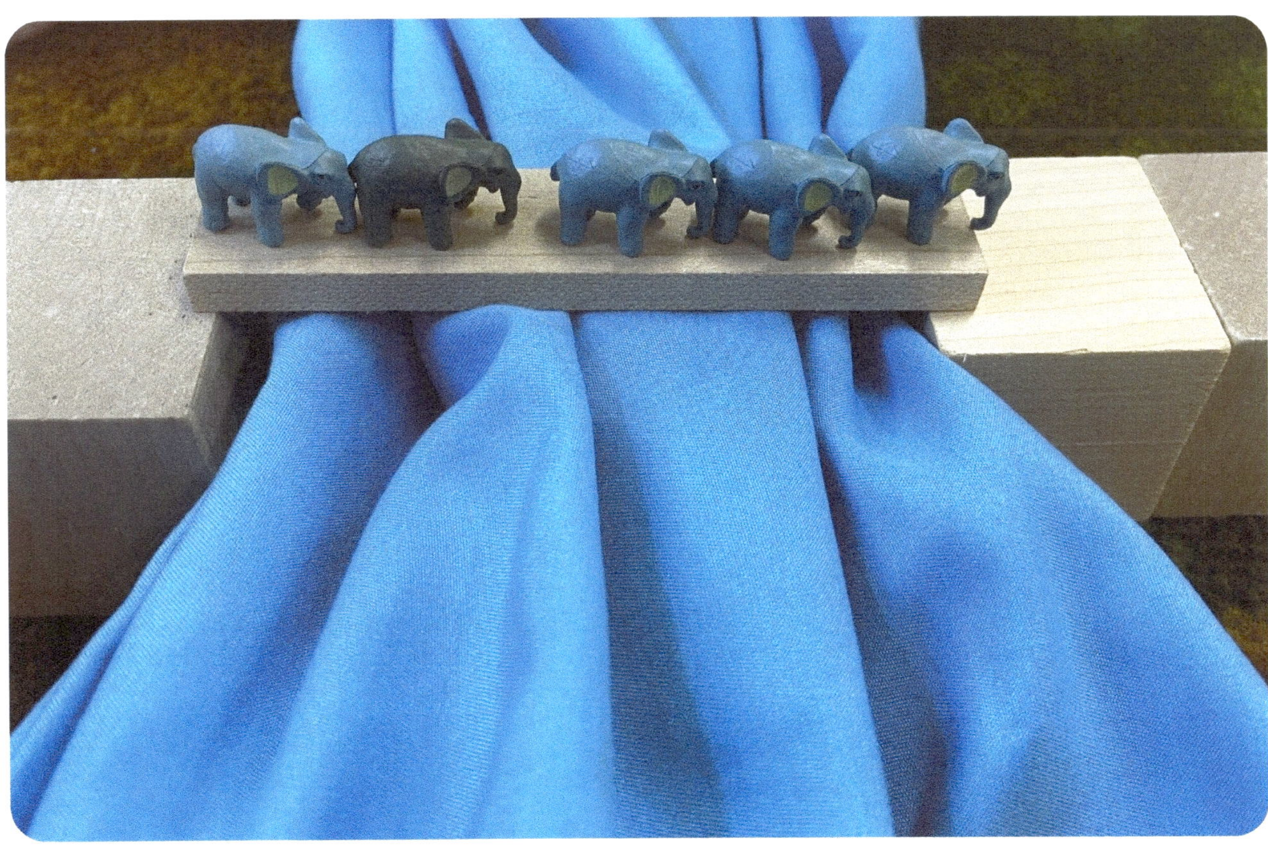

Document

Create a list or chart that documents how many animals each bridge was able to hold. Take photos of each bridge or invite children to draw a sketch of their bridge design.

Reflect

Ask children to consider how they might make their bridges even stronger next time.

Think Ahead

Given the opportunity to build with blocks and other construction materials, children are often inspired to build structures that mirror those they see in their own community as well as those they see in books and other media. Many of these structures have an important purpose: to help people travel and live safely with bodies of water. As we explored in this chapter, bridges, canals, and tunnels are just a few of the structures humans engineer that are related to water. In our next chapter, we'll sharpen our focus on more human-made systems, including the pipes and plumbing you find in the walls of your own home.

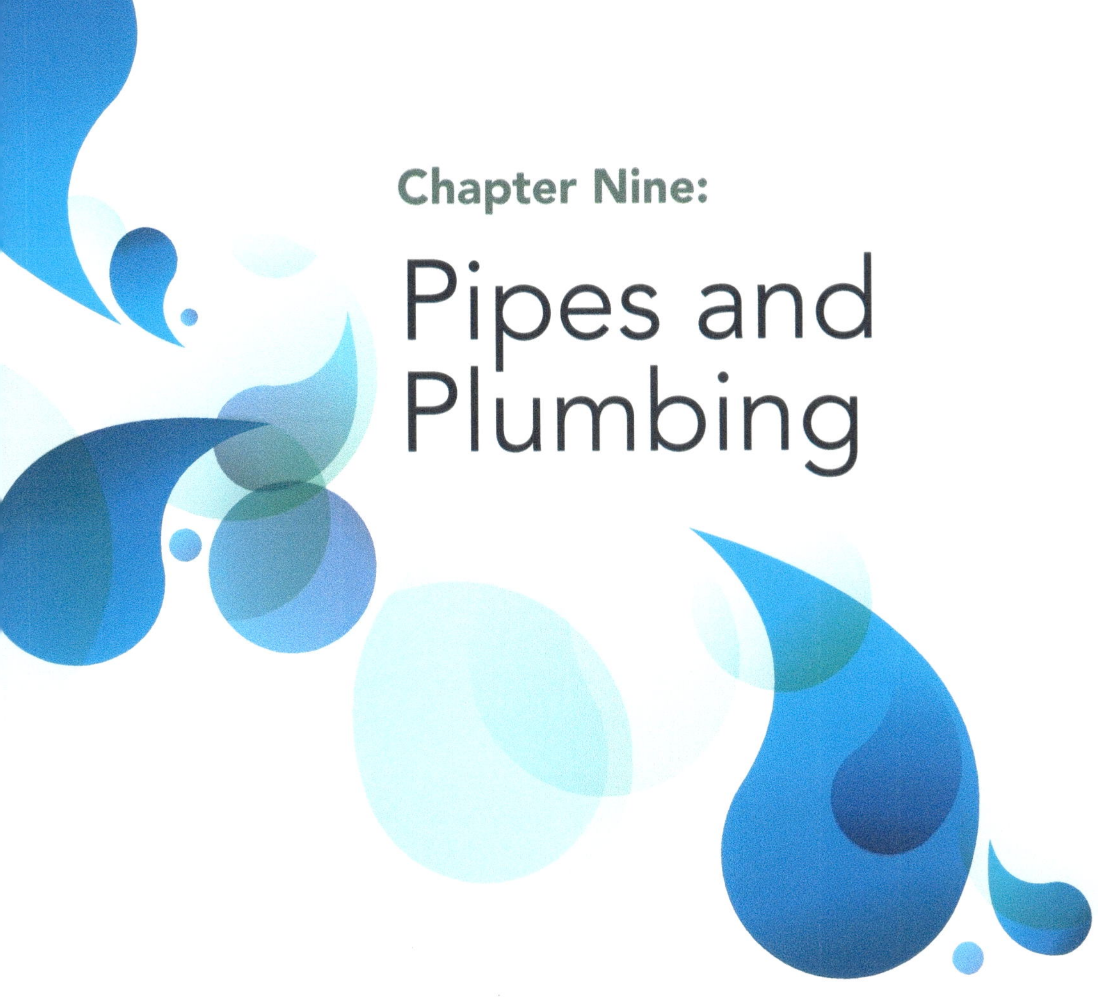

Chapter Nine:

Pipes and Plumbing

It's almost snack time in Ms. Amy's preschool class, and the children are taking turns washing hands. "You're next, Olivia," says Ms. Amy, gesturing to the classroom sink.

Three-year-old Olivia moves toward the sink, but instead of stepping up on the little stool, she crawls under the sink.

"Hmm," says Ms. Amy. "I see you under the sink, Olivia. What are you doing down there?"

Olivia says, "Watching the drip."

"Watching the drip?" says Ms. Amy. "What is dripping?"

"The leak," says Olivia. "The leak is leaking."

Ms. Amy sees the other children waiting to wash their hands and sighs. "Olivia," says Ms. Amy, "I'm going to let someone else wash their hands while you're looking at the leak."

"Okay!" says Olivia.

First Benji, then Dylan, then Maya wash their hands, and still Olivia stays under the sink. "Olivia," says Ms. Amy, "it's time to come out now and wash your hands." Olivia does not move.

"Olivia, I don't want you to miss eating your snack. Come out now and we can check the leak after snack is over."

Olivia scoots out from under the sink and starts washing her hands. "I want to watch the leak after snack."

"Okay," says Ms. Amy. "Let's put this flat tray under the pipe to catch the drips. We'll look again after snack. What do you think we'll see?"

"More drips," says Olivia. "Drip, drip, drip."

As the children eat snack, Ms. Amy wonders why Olivia is so interested in the leaky pipe under the sink. She decides to call her brother-in-law Nick, a plumber, and ask him about what causes pipes to leak. She wonders if Nick might be able to come and visit her class and talk about how pipes and plumbing work.

Almost every school setting in the United States has a system of pipes and plumbing available for children to observe as part of their daily routines. (The exception might be outdoor classrooms such as forest preschools.) As illustrated in the scenario above, children are often curious about how things work, especially the sinks, faucets, and other devices they use multiple times every day. Children wonder where the water comes from and where it goes after it flows down the drain. They're curious about the curvy twists and turns of the pipes they can observe under sinks. Children also enjoy opportunities to learn about how things work, how they break or leak, and how they can be fixed.

The content of this chapter focuses on one specific category of the built environment—pipes, plumbing, and the infrastructure involved in moving clean water into our homes and buildings.

Learning Objectives

In the context of scientific reasoning, the movement of water through pipes in a home or school serves as an important "observable phenomenon." The significance of observing, discussing, and documenting phenomena is represented in the goals of the Head Start Early Learning Outcomes Framework.

Head Start Early Learning Outcomes Framework

Goal P-SCI 3. Child compares and categorizes observable phenomena.

Uses measurement tools, such as a ruler, balance scale, eye dropper, unit blocks, thermometer, or measuring cup, to quantify similarities and differences of observable phenomena. (U.S. Department of Health and Human Services, Administration for Children and Families, Office of Head Start, 2015).

Additionally, plumbing and pipe systems are examples of civil engineering projects. The process of defining and considering engineering problem is prioritized in the Next Generation Science Standards (NGSS) as disciplinary core ideas.

Next Generation Science Standards

Engineering, Technology, and Applications of Science

ETS1.A Defining Engineering Problems

A situation that people want to change or create can be approached as a problem to be solved through engineering. Such problems may have many acceptable solutions.

ETS1.A Defining and Delimiting an Engineering Problem

Asking questions, making observations, and gathering information are helpful in thinking about problems (National Research Council, 2013).

Another interesting topic related to pipes and plumbing is the physics concept of gravity. Gravity is not typically taught in preschool, but young children are certainly capable of understanding that water flows down, not up. Gravity is essential to how household plumbing works, as it drives the movement of water and waste through pipes and drains.

NAEYC accreditation standards refer to physics and the solving of problems.

NAEYC Early Learning Program Accreditation Standards and Assessment Items

Topic 2.G Science

Young children begin learning science concepts when they use their senses explore objects in the environment, make things happen, and solve problems (NAEYC, 2022).

Based on these references and priorities in the Head Start framework, NGSS, and NAEYC accreditation standards, the following are developmentally informed and responsive objectives related to pipes and plumbing. These four objectives are worded and structured in ways that help you scaffold children's learning experiences, provide meaningful, play-based contexts for learning, and create foundations for future learning.

Chapter 9 Learning Objectives

1. Support children's growing understanding of pipes, plumbing, and the ways water moves through a built environment.
2. Provide opportunities for children to observe and discuss pipes and plumbing in the built environment.
3. During regular water play and construction play, indoors and outdoors, expose children to play experiences and challenges that allow children to explore and discover how to build structures that move water.
4. Conduct teacher-facilitated science experiments that demonstrate and test different ways of moving water through pipes.

Background Information for Educators

How does plumbing work? In a nutshell, some pipes bring clean water in, and others take dirty water out. The process gets a bit more complicated when you look at the specific fixtures and appliances in your home that help make that happen. And things get even more complicated when you look beyond your house, at your community's water systems, to how water is processed to ensure it is clean before it enters your home, and at how wastewater is removed to ensure its safe disposal.

Vocabulary

Pipe: a long, hollow tube for carrying a liquid or gas

Plumbing: a system of pipes and fixtures that carries water through a building

Drain: a device that is used remove or draw away liquid

Faucet: a device that is used for regulating the flow of water, usually from a pipe

Valve: a mechanical device that opens and closes, controlling the flow of a liquid or gas

Pump: a device that moves a liquid or gas

Sewer: a device, usually underground, that is used to carry off water and sewage

Sewage: waste matter that is carried away from homes and other locations

Let's start inside your home. You may already have some knowledge of plumbing systems and how water moves through the pipes in your home. Perhaps you've learned by necessity how to fix a leaky pipe or unclog a bathtub drain. There is a wealth of information online for do-it-yourselfers and fixer-uppers that can be helpful to educators as we explore these topics with children. Here are a few helpful resources:

"How Your House Plumbing Works"
https://www.youtube.com/watch?v=SsPtZqOAf4s

"Plumbing Basics"
https://home.howstuffworks.com/home-improvement/plumbing/plumbing-basics-ga.htm

DIY Plumbing
https://www.homedepot.com/c/alp/home-improvement-ideas-diy-plumbing/dqe7-7lff

Outside your home, community water systems provide clean water to homes and businesses and ensure that wastewater is removed safely. Check the website of your local government (city or county) to find out more about how your water is processed. For example, in the Chicago area the Metropolitan Water Reclamation District of Greater Chicago (MWRD) is responsible for treating wastewater and providing stormwater management for residents and businesses. MWRD provides a virtual tour that explains what they do (see https://www.youtube.com/watch?v=__yXMrBYek4).

Another great video resource comes from the Metropolitan Council of the Twin Cities in Minnesota: "The Metropolitan Council presents Wastewater Treatment for Kids."
https://www.youtube.com/watch?v=DDbNeAfclOU

Ask a Water Scientist

Can toilet water be cleaned up and used again as drinking water?

Yes, and it is! There is a finite amount of water on Earth, so it's essential that we reuse water. In most areas of the United States, the water that comes out of our taps has been through many different processes that ensure it is clean and ready to drink.

For example, water treatment plants take water from groundwater sources, lakes, or rivers and filter it using gravel or sand to remove particles from the water. They also add chemicals such as chlorine to kill germs (Tan, 2016). Once the water is clean, it can be transported through pipes to homes and businesses. In some places where water supplies are more limited, such as Orange County, California, wastewater treatments systems have been developed to clean water that comes from sewage systems—water from toilets—into water that is safe to drink. Extra water sanitation steps, such as zapping the water with ultraviolet light, ensure that the water is clean and safe for drinking (Ingebretsen, n.d.).

Explore

Inviting and exploring children's interests around plumbing and water systems is relatively easy because pipes and plumbing can probably be observed all around the school. When children turn on the taps in the sink to wash their hands, ask, "Where does the water come from?" or simply muse, "I wonder where the water comes from..." and see how they respond. If they answer, "From the pipes!" ask, "How do you know?" and "Where do the pipes get the water?"

Go on a pipe hunt in your school. Visit the bathrooms, kitchens, and anywhere there might be a sink or some form of plumbing. Take pictures, make a list, and invite the children to draw pictures of what you see. If possible, visit the basement or utility closets and observe other parts of the plumbing system, such as water heaters.

Invite the janitor, facility manager, or a local plumber to visit your class and answer children's questions about the water systems in your building.

Read aloud *How Does Plumbing Work?* by Elizabeth Andrews, and make a list of additional questions children might like to explore.

Play

Children can explore concepts of plumbing and water systems through play, with or without water. During water play, in sensory tables or bins, invite children to play with pipes of different shapes and sizes. Use real pipes (such as PVC pipes), toy pipe construction sets, plastic straws, or pieces of hose. I like using pieces from plastic marble runs in the sensory table; many of the pipes, gutters, and funnels used in marble play can be safely used with water.

Children can also build pipe systems without real water. They can join paper towel tubes together with tape to create connecting shapes and pathways. Construction toys like Straws and Connectors can also be used for plumbing-inspired play. Join dollhouses and doll furniture, such as little sinks and toilets, using paper or plastic straws that look like plumbing systems. Straws can also be added to the block corner, where children can build homes and other buildings, complete with a utility infrastructure that brings clean water in and takes dirty water out.

Recommended Children's Books

***A Plumber's Job* by Niles Worthington**

Part of a nonfiction series about community helpers, this book describes the duties of a plumber and the tools they use.

***Curious George, Plumber's Helper* by H.A. Rey**

Curious George learns a lesson about how plumbing works when he tries to help fix a clogged pipe. This book also includes some nonfiction facts and explanations about how plumbing systems work.

***How It Works: Toilets* by Tracy Abell**

This book is part of a series of eight STEM books called How It Works. The text is informative but probably not suitable for a group read-aloud. The pictures, however, will spark a lot of great conversation and questions.

Experiment

Activity: Fix That Leak!

I discovered that many children are excited and fascinated by leaky pipes when I introduced my class to the card game *Water Works* by Winning Moves Games. Although this is a strategy game designed for children ages eight and older, I simplified the game by making it a cooperative project. Each card is illustrated with a section of pipe with some intact and others leaking drops of water. I handed out one card to each child and invited them to take turns adding their card to create a connected system of pipes. If one of the cards showed a leaky pipe, they could "fix" the leak by laying a card on top of it, as long as the shape of the new pipe matched the leaky pipe. The children loved the suspense and drama of the question "Who can fix the leaky pipe?" We continued through the deck of cards, each taking a turn, until all the leaks were fixed and they had created a connected pathway of pipes across the floor.

Prepare

Materials: sensory table or bin, water, PVC pipes or toy pipes

Create a similar challenge with real water in a sensory table or bin. Set up a set of PVC pipes or toy pipes in a way that allows for a significant water leak. Then invite children to take turns solving the problem and fixing the leak.

Observe and Experiment

Demonstrate the leaky pipes by pouring water through the construction of pipes. Ask children to identify the location of the leak. Then ask, "How can we solve this problem?"

Allow children to brainstorm multiple solutions. Some solutions might be pretend or fanciful, but others will likely be more practical and workable.

Strategies might include the following:

- Add some tape
- Stop up the leak with some bubble gum
- Tighten up the pipes
- Use different pipes
- Pour the water more slowly

Test different solutions and observe what happens. Was the leak fixed?

Document

Document children's initial ideas and solutions on a piece of paper or whiteboard. Then take notes as they play and test their ideas. Ask, "What did you try?" and "What happened?" Write down their words and observations.

Reflect

Talk about what worked and what didn't work. Invite children to use what they learned from this experiment in their play. For example, if the children learn that paper straws tend to break, tear, and leak, invite them to try using plastic straws during water play. Which materials had the most leaks? How do you know?

Think Ahead

Learning about household plumbing and our water systems is closely connected to the content of the previous chapter and the next chapter. As always, follow the children's lead and let their interests guide you as you make decisions about the path of your curriculum.

Chapter Ten: Where Does Water Come From?

It's free-play time in Ms. Jenna's preschool class, and she has offered the children a set of colorful teapots, teacups, and teaspoons to use in the sensory table, which is filled with several inches of water. A small group of children pretends to have a tea party. They are filling the teapots with water and pouring the water into the teacups.

Henry says, "Look, Maria, I'm adding some sugar to my tea." Henry uses a spoon to stir the water in his teacup.

Maria says, "My tea is too hot. I'm blowing on it."

Henry holds the teacup to his mouth and takes a sip of water.

Maria says, "Eww! Don't drink it."

"It's just water!" protests Henry.

Maria says, "It's dirty water."

Ms. Jenna adds, "Let's just pretend to drink the tea."

You can hardly blame Henry for wanting to take a sip of the water in the sensory table. It looked clear and clean. And the teacup is exactly like the cups his mother uses to drink her tea every morning. In this chapter, we'll explore ways to explain to children how to know if water is safe to drink. But to do that, we also need to talk about the water cycle—the process our Earth uses to recycle and reuse water over and over and over again.

Learning Objectives

When considering developmentally appropriate learning objectives related to exploring the importance of clean and safe water, it makes sense to consider how young children learn concepts of basic health and hygiene. In fact, many of the goals from the Head Start Early Learning Outcomes Framework are connected to the importance of staying clean and safe. For example, the goal "Child demonstrates personal hygiene and self-care skills" includes the indicator "Washes hands with soap and water."

Head Start Early Learning Outcomes Framework

Goal P-PMP 4. Child demonstrates personal hygiene and self-care skills.

Washes hands with soap and water. Knows to do this before eating, after using the bathroom, or after blowing nose.

Goal P-PMP 6. Child demonstrates knowledge of personal safety practices and routines.

Identifies, avoids, and alerts others to danger, such as keeping a safe distance from swings.

Identifies and follows basic safety rules with adult guidance and support, such as transportation and street safety practices (Department of Health and Human Services, Administration for Children and Families, Office of Head Start, 2015).

Exploring concepts of clean and safe water also involves learning about the science behind the water cycle—the idea that our resources are valuable and limited. We can look to Next Generation Science Standards for guidance on how to frame learning objectives related to natural resources.

Next Generation Science Standards

ESS3.A Natural Resources

Living things need water, air, and resources from the land, and they live in places that have the things they need. Humans use natural resources for everything they do (National Research Council, 2013).

We can create developmentally informed and responsive learning objectives that address these two separate but related categories—physical health and safety, along with the science of natural resources. The following four objectives are worded and structured in ways that help you scaffold children's learning experiences, provide meaningful, play-based contexts for learning, and create foundations for future learning.

Chapter 10 Learning Objectives

1. Support children's growing understanding of the importance of water.
2. Provide opportunities for children to observe and discuss the water cycle.
3. During regular water play and dramatic play indoors and outdoors, expose children to experiences that help them make connections between their own use of clean water and the Earth's water cycle.
4. Conduct teacher-facilitated science activities and experiments that demonstrate the water cycle and the importance of clean and safe water.

Background Information for Educators

All the Water in the World by George Ella Lyon is among my favorite picture books about water. It begins with these words:

"All the water in the world is all the water in the world."

This means that the Earth is not getting any new water, and the water we have is not going anywhere. All the water in the world is, indeed, all the water in the world.

According to the United States Geological Survey (2024), we have almost 1.4 billion cubic kilometers of water, including oceans, glaciers, groundwater, streams, lakes—everything! This water is recycled by nature over and over again in a process called the water cycle.

Our water is constantly moving through a cycle that includes evaporation, condensation, precipitation, and collection (Britannica Kids, n.d.).

The Water Cycle

The water on Earth and in the atmosphere exists in three primary forms—liquid, solid (ice), and gas (steam, fog, clouds, and so on). Water is constantly moving through these states. The way water changes states and moves around Earth is called the water cycle.

Here's how that works. When the liquid water found in places like oceans and rivers gets warm, it forms a gas. That's called *evaporation*. The water vapor forms clouds. When the water vapor (gas) cools, the water returns to a liquid state, often through rain. That's called *condensation*. Another part of the water cycle is the movement of liquid water to solid water, as ice. Water vapor can also freeze to become snow (National Oceanic and Atmospheric Administration, 2023).

Vocabulary

Evaporation: to change from a liquid into a vapor

Condensation: the process by which a gas or vapor cools and becomes a liquid

Cycle: a process or series of events that leads back to the beginning

Gas: a substance (such as steam) that has no fixed shape and tends to expand

Vapor: the gas form of a substance such as water

The water cycle describes how nature recycles water. When you drink a glass of water, that water is made up of molecules that have been traveling over the Earth for centuries in many different forms. It can be fun to think that you're drinking water that was perhaps once snow at the North Pole or maybe rain that fell on the African savanna. On the other hand, from a health and sanitation perspective, it can be disconcerting to think that we bathe in and drink water that has been in so many different places. It's a good thing that human innovation and technology provide ways to clean water.

As mentioned in the previous chapter, the water that comes into our home for bathing, drinking, and cooking has been cleaned and processed. For more information about how we ensure our water is safe to drink, here are a few educational resources.

"How the Water You Flush Becomes the Water You Drink"
https://www.youtube.com/watch?v=SYia4zqcE4g

"Magic of Making—A Drink from the Tap"
https://www.youtube.com/watch?v=Zsb2bim2Kn0&t=47s

While these videos are intended for elementary and middle-grade students, they can be helpful for adults as well, as we enrich our own content knowledge and confidence about how water is processed.

Explore

The picture book quoted previously, *All the Water in the World* by George Ella Lyon, describes the water cycle with colorful illustrations and simple explanations. I especially enjoy using this book on a rainy day, as I invite children to think about where the raindrops come from.

- Asking open-ended questions sparks fascinating conversations related to the water cycle:
- Where does the rain come from?
- Clouds? Well, what are the clouds made out of?
- How does the rainwater get into the clouds?
- What happens to the rain after it falls? Where does it go?
- How do you know?

A prop such as a clear jar filled with water, along with a ball to represent the Earth, helps to illustrate that there is a fixed amount of water on and around our planet.

Another option for sparking interest in the water cycle is music. A band called The Bazillions has recorded a wonderful song and video about the water cycle (see https://www.youtube.com/watch?v=DJBXflNyFs4&t=5s).

Keep in mind that we are simply exposing children to the concept of the water cycle, a topic they will study in greater detail when they are older. For now, the primary message to young children is that our water supply is limited, not endless, so we must be careful to take care of our water (and each other).

Recommended Children's Books

***Drop: An Adventure through the Water Cycle* by Emily Kate Moon**

An adorable drop of water makes her way through the water cycle, demonstrating the various states of matter using delightful illustrations and fun language.

***Raindrops Roll* by April Pulley Sayre**

Vibrant, close-up photographs of raindrops in the natural world are paired with simple and lyrical explanations of rain's role in the water cycle.

***Water Is Water* by Miranda Paul**

This nonfiction picture is also included in chapter 1 as a great read-aloud when introducing children to water topics. It can be helpful to revisit this book when discussing the water cycle and the ways water changes from gas to liquid to solid, and from solid to liquid again.

All the water in the world
by George Ella Lyon and Katherine Tillotson
LIBYA
SUDAN
ALGERIA

Play

Rather than suggesting specific water play activities in this chapter, let's explore ways children can be involved in the setting up and cleaning up of water play activities. It is through their direct experience with accessing water and disposing of water that children will expand their understanding of where our water comes from and our responsibility for keeping our water clean and safe.

Setup and Cleanup

Assisting in the setup and cleanup of water play activities can be a rotating helper position. Invite one or two children to assist a teacher in adding clean water to the sensory table or water bin. Ask the water helpers to check the toys and containers first to ensure that everything is clean and ready. Then include children in the process of adding water. If water must be carried from one part of the room to another, the children will soon discover that water is heavy! Using small buckets with handles allows children to participate with some independence.

Children may suggest adding more and more water to containers. Ask children to consider, "How much water do we really need?"

Afterward, during cleanup, involve children in the emptying of the water play containers. As part of this process, discuss where the water will go next.

"Can this water be saved for drinking or cooking? Why not?"

"If we pour this water down the drain, where will it go next?"

Experiment

Activity: Filter Dirty Water

Prepare

Materials: a pitcher of water, two bowls, two sieves or colanders that will fit each bowl, paper coffee filters, large spoon, a few cups of dirt or potting soil, a large bucket

In this facilitated experiment, children will take turns adding dirt to water and then pouring it through two types of filters. Children will observe and reflect on which filtering tools work best to clean the water.

To prepare, you will need a bucket or pitcher of water (preferably clear, so children can see how dirty the water gets) and a sieve or colander that fits into the opening of a bowl that will catch the filtered water. Ideally, it's nice to have two sieves in two bowls: one with just the sieve and one with both the sieve and a coffee filter. This way, you can compare how the water looks after filtering

with just the sieve to how the water looks after filtering with both the sieve and the coffee filter. You will also need a big spoon for stirring, a small amount of dirt (such as potting soil), and some paper coffee filters. And you will need a bucket or container to use for disposing of the dirty water after each step in the experiment.

Observe and Experiment

Work with children in pairs or small groups. If possible, take photos of each step in the process.

First, have children take turns adding some dirt to the water in the bucket or pitcher. Invite children to observe how the color and appearance of the water changes as the dirt is added.

Then have children take turns pouring some of the dirty water through the sieve and observing what happens. The children will likely observe that the water is still quite dirty. The sieve only removes bigger chunks of dirt or stones. Then compare this outcome to what happens when dirty water is poured through both the sieve and several layers of paper coffee filters. Children will be able to see that even though the water is still dirty, it is much cleaner than when you used just the sieve.

Document

Take photos and/or notes before, during, and after the experiment. Write down children's questions and comments. You'll be able to use this documentation afterward to share with the children and help them reflect on the process. You can also share this documentation with parents and family members.

Reflect

Ask children, "Would you want to drink this water?" Remind children that the water we drink has gone through a special process that works much better than the tools we use in this experiment.

This experiment can also be done outdoors, which can help avoid some concerns about spills and messes. If time, space, and materials allow, give children the opportunity to play with and experiment with these materials in an open-ended way.

Activity: Observe a Terrarium

Prepare

A terrarium is a sealable container, usually glass, in which houseplants can grow. A terrarium garden is easy to maintain because it waters itself. The seal or lid on the terrarium keeps the moisture inside. The warmth of the sun causes the water in the soil to evaporate. The water vapor (gas) created by the evaporation then condenses on the glass surface and drips back into the soil. The terrarium is self-watering because it creates its own water cycle.

Observing a terrarium, especially over a period of many days, is a great opportunity to observe a water cycle. You can find many resources on how to make a terrarium online (see, for example, https://www.thespruce.com/how-to-make-terrariums-848007).

Observe and Experiment

Create an observation station next to the terrarium. Set up chairs or cushions that allow for one or two children to sit and watch the terrarium.

Explain to children that the plants in the terrarium already have all the water they need inside their home. Invite children to watch how the water moves up (through evaporation) and down (through condensation).

Occasionally, the plants in a terrarium will need additional water, especially if the container is not fully sealed. Ask the children to help you decide when the terrarium is getting too dry. Do they still see evidence of drops (condensation) on the roof and sides of the terrarium? Does the soil look lighter or drier? Are any leaves on the plants turning brown? This could mean a little water is needed. Invite children to help water the inside using a spray bottle or mister.

Document

Provide paper and pencils on clipboards that children can use to write or draw what they see. Invite children to draw what they see inside the terrarium and encourage them to focus on one interesting thing to draw, such as a particular leaf. Label children's drawings with the day or date. Explain that observing and drawing what they see is something that scientists do to record how things change over time. Post the drawings in order, to create a timeline showing how the terrarium looks over several days. Don't worry if children's drawings are not precise or accurate. They are practicing skills that they will continue to develop as they grow older.

Reflect

Ask children to think about how a terrarium is the same and different from the nature they see outside in parks and gardens. How is the rain in a terrarium different from the rain that falls from the sky? How is it the same? Older children (kindergarten and above) may be able to understand that the Earth has an atmosphere that acts like the roof of a terrarium, holding water, in the form of vapor, clouds, and precipitation, close to the Earth.

Think Ahead

These ideas and activities in this chapter build on the content of the previous chapters, challenging children to think creatively about where our water comes from and where it goes after we use it. In the next chapter, we'll explore ways to dive even deeper into water conservation and protecting our environment and our natural resources.

Chapter Eleven:

Caring for Water and Our Planet

Ms. Laura's preschool class is preparing for snack. Some of the children are washing hands at the classroom sink and others are helping Ms. Laura and her co-teacher, Mr. James, place cups and napkins on the tables.

Four-year-olds Jasmine and Will are sharing the sink as they wash their hands. Will has his hand on the cold water handle as Jasmine rubs her hands with soap.

"Stop it!" yells Jasmine. "I'm not done."

"I know!" says Will.

Jasmine starts to cry, and Ms. Laura moves closer.

"I heard you crying, Jasmine," says Ms. Laura. "What's going on?"

"I'm not done!" wails Jasmine. "He's not letting me wash!"

"She's using too much water," says Will. "She's wasting it."

Ms. Laura asks, "Will, why do you think Jasmine is wasting water?"

Will starts to cry now too. "Because all the water is going down the drain and she's not even touching it!"

Ms. Laura says, "I think I understand. Let's work this out." She helps Jasmine rinse her hands and pulls up a chair. The teacher sits with both children until they've both stopped crying and calmed down. "It sounds like Jasmine was washing her hands and making sure her fingers got nice and soapy." Jasmine nods. "And then, Will noticed that the water was running without anybody using it to rinse. So you turned off the water, right, Will? But then Jasmine needed the water to rinse her hands, and she couldn't because the water was off." Will nods. "I think it's good to save water when we can. Will, you have some good ideas about that." Will smiles. "But Jasmine needed water to rinse and she also needed to be in charge of her own handwashing. Is that right, Jasmine?"

Jasmine nods and says, "I can do my own water."

"Yes," says Ms. Laura. "You can do your own water."

Ms. Laura turns to Will and says, "Let's think of some other ways we can remind people to take care of our water and not waste it."

Will says, "We could make a sign."

"That's a great idea, Will. Let's do that. And let's keep thinking of other ways to save water."

Once children begin really thinking about the importance of clean water in their lives, they may sometimes surprise us with the intensity of their efforts to do the right thing. As illustrated in the scenario above, Will was so focused on conserving water that he tried to take charge of other children's handwashing efforts.

It's important that children are exposed to many different ideas and approaches to caring for water, our natural environment, and our Earth's resources. In this chapter, we'll explore developmentally appropriate environmental science and conservation activities. Our broad goal is to emphasize the important role of children, families, and communities in working together to protect our planet and our most valuable resource: water.

Learning Objectives

Although water protection and water conservation fall under the category of environmental science, these ideas are probably best understood by young children as forms of care. We care for ourselves and for each other by making sure we have clean water for drinking, bathing, and cleaning. We care for fish and other animals by keeping our oceans clean. We care for our whole planet—for animals and insects, for plants and trees, for people everywhere—by using only what we need and not wasting our natural resources.

Environmentally responsible practices are included in NAEYC accreditation standards. For example:

NAEYC Early Learning Program Accreditation Standards and Assessment Items

Topic 2.L Social Studies

Preschool and kindergarten children are ready to engage in discussions about fairness, friendship, responsibility, authority, and differences... children can learn how people affect their environment in positive ways (e.g., recycling) and negative ways (e.g., polluting). Environmentally responsible practices are reinforced when the program creates opportunities to educate families as well as children on eco-healthy practices such as the importance of washing fruits and vegetables before eating them, using non-toxic toys and art supplies, monitoring outdoor air quality, and using least-toxic and fragrance free cleaning products (NAEYC, 2022).

Caring for the Earth and each other is also a common theme in Next Generation Science Standards.

Next Generation Science Standards

K-ESS2 Earth's Systems

ESS3.C Human Impacts on Earth Systems

Things that people do to live comfortably can affect the world around them. But they can make choices that reduce their impacts on the land, water, air, and other living things.

K-ESS3 Earth and Human Activity

K-ESS3-3 Communicate solutions that will reduce the impact of humans on the land, water, air, and/or other living things in the local environment.

ESS3.A Natural Resources

Living things need water, air, and resources from the land, and they live in places that have the things they need. Humans use natural resources for everything they do (National Research Council, 2013).

Informed by these resources, the following three objectives shape our approach to teaching young children to care for water and our planet. These objectives are worded and structured in ways that help you scaffold children's learning experiences, provide meaningful, play-based contexts for learning, and create foundations for future learning.

Chapter 11 Learning Objectives

1. Support children's growing understanding of water as an essential resource.
2. Provide opportunities for children, along with their families, to discuss how we can help protect and care for our planet's natural resources.
3. During regular water play and dramatic play indoors and outdoors, expose children to concepts related to water conservation and environmental protection.

Background Information for Educators

The importance of protecting our natural resources, especially water, is growing due to threats from pollution and climate change. For example, pollution from chemicals creates "hotspots" in rivers worldwide, harming ecosystems and making water unsafe for people (Keegan, 2021). And there is increasing concern about microplastics in drinking water (Borenstein, 2024). Another significant factor is climate change, which amplifies water problems by intensifying droughts and floods. Rising global temperatures make droughts more common in some areas while increasing rain and flooding in others. Extreme weather events impact both the access to water and the quality of the water supply (Earth Day, 2020).

Vocabulary

Drought: a prolonged time of dryness, often caused by lack of rain

Extreme weather events: occurrences of unusually severe weather or climate conditions that may cause damage to communities and ecosystems (U.S. Department of Agriculture, n.d.)

Hydrology: the scientific study of Earth's water (National Oceanic and Atmospheric Administration, 2025)

Natural resources: materials supplied by nature that are used by people, such as water, wood, or coal

Sea level rise: an increase in the level of the world's oceans due to the effects of global warming (National Geographic Society, 2023)

Water conservation: the practice of using water efficiently to reduce waste (Constellation, 2025)

While it's important for adults to understand the significant issues impacting our climate, our environment, and our water supply, it would not be appropriate to share this complex information with children. We, as educators, can use this information to motivate us to be active supporters of and advocates for our environment and teach children to respect and protect our natural resources.

Ask a Water Scientist

What are some actions we can take now that will help us protect water resources in the future?

Learn about your own water resources. Where does your water come from? Where is the closest water treatment facility to your house? You can usually find this on your local government's website or by contacting your local water supplier.

Follow your community's guidelines on when and how much to water your lawn and avoid using harmful pesticides that could drain into local water supplies. In general, proper disposal of chemicals is important to keep our waterways clean. Volunteering at an event like a beach cleanup can be a fun way to get out in your community to help clean up your local water supply while also learning more about it.

There are several organizations in the United States dedicated to advocating for the protection of the environment and water resources. These include:

- **Waterkeeper Alliance** https://waterkeeper.org/
- **National Association of Clean Water Agencies** https://www.nacwa.org/
- **Friends of the Earth** https://foe.org/
- **The Nature Conservancy** https://www.nature.org/en-us/

Explore

To build interest and engagement in the topic of water protection, think about a real issue in your school community and how to connect children to that issue in ways that are developmentally appropriate and meaningful to children.

What are the water issues in your own community? Has the community experienced any extreme weather that has resulted in flooding or drought? Are there any current issues related to protecting natural habitats, parks, or recreation areas? Are any of the parents or family members in your community involved in environmental issues?

Once you target an environmental issue, such as pollution in a local river, that you think the children might respond to, consider who you might invite to visit your school to help explain and demonstrate the issue. Some possible roles might include the following:

- Environmental scientist
- Water resource engineer
- Water treatment plant operator
- Water quality specialist
- Water conservation specialist
- Aquatic ecologist
- Stormwater manager

As mentioned, your local government agencies may be good resources for finding someone to visit your school. Ask your guest to bring photos, posters, or tools to help the children understand their work. Invite parents and family members to participate in the visit.

Another way to spark children's interest in protecting the environment and our water resources is through stories. *We Are the Water Protectors* by Carole Lindstrom is an award-winning picture book that describes the work of Indigenous communities to protect their land and water.

Another book by the same author, *Autumn Peltier, Water Warrior,* celebrates a real-life water activist. Finally, *The Water Princess* by Susan Verde is inspired by a true story of the struggle to access clean drinking water in an African community. See Recommended Picture Books for additional sources.

On a similar note, this short video about the Warka Water Towers demonstrates a positive and innovative approach to ensuring that everyone has access to clean water:

"Warka Water Towers Harvest Drinkable Water from the Air" https://www.youtube.com/watch?v=THJVuinPbc0

Recommended Picture Books

***We Need Water* by Charles Ghigna**

It's hard to find environmental science books that are appropriate for young children, but *We Need Water* is a rare find. The rhyming text is fun and easy to read aloud, and the message is simple and direct: We all can help keep our water clean because we all need water.

***The Water Lady: How Darlene Arviso Helps a Thirsty Navajo Nation* by Alice B. McGinty**

This picture book tells the true story of a Navajo woman, Darlene Arviso, and her hard work to deliver water to a native community with few options for obtaining clean drinking water.

***One Turtle's Last Straw: The Real-Life Rescue That Sparked a Sea Change* by Elisa Boxer**

This picture book is based on a true story about the impact of plastics on our oceans and the creatures that live there. In this case, an endangered sea turtle is rescued after a discarded plastic straw becomes stuck in its nose. The book provides a clear message that people must do more to keep our oceans clean.

***Great Lakes: Our Freshwater Treasure* by Barb Rosenstock**

Whether you live near the shores of the Great Lakes or not, the text and images in *Great Lakes: Our Freshwater Treasure* provide a clear picture of the importance of fresh water to people, animals, and the environment. This well-researched picture book includes information from and about Indigenous communities.

Play

All the play ideas presented in this book can be supported and facilitated in ways that teach and model care for our planet. Whenever children play with water or use natural resources as part of their play, encourage them to use only what they need and to avoid waste. Ordinary classroom routines, like cleaning up the classroom and washing hands, are opportunities to demonstrate and talk about how grateful we are for what we have—not just the water we use but also the paper we draw on, the toys we play with, the snack eat, as well as the friends and teachers and neighbors who help us every day. When playing outdoors, observe and talk about the plants, birds, and other animals that live in the natural environment and the importance of keeping it clean and safe for all living things.

Experiment

Caring for water and our planet is more important than one standalone science experiment; it is something we all can do every day. Instead of offering ideas for science experiments, here is a list of suggested actions that can be included as a regular part of an early childhood classroom routine.

1. **Save water.** Teach children to turn off the faucet when they are finished washing their hands.
2. **Plant a classroom garden.** Indoors, terrariums and pots can be used to grow houseplants or herbs. Outdoors, a raised bed or tilled area can be used to grow flowers or vegetables. Children can help plan, plant, and tend the garden.
3. **Water plants wisely.** Show children how to water plants using only what's needed—not too much and not too little. Also, have children collect rainwater in containers outdoors and use that to water plants at school.
4. **Clean up outdoor spaces.** During outdoor walks and playtimes, involve children in the process of picking up litter. Model how to use gloves or tongs to safely pick up and dispose of items.
5. **Encourage the use of reusable water bottles and food containers.** As a school and as a staff, model the use of reusable containers such as water bottles. Explain to children and families how this practice saves resources and benefits the environment.
6. **Recycle classroom items.** If your school does not participate in a recycling program, start one in your classroom. Research the recycling options available in your community and begin collecting items that children can easily identify, such as paper and cardboard.
7. **Compost food waste.** Like recycling, composting demonstrates care for our environment by showing children how to make the most of our resources. Research the composting options available in your community and start small by composting waste that children can safely collect at school, such as orange peels and apple cores.

A Final Note of Hope

The water science ideas and activities presented in this book each began with sparks of curiosity and the joy of play. In my direct experience working with children on this curriculum, I sought to follow the children's interests and excitement. Whether the children are exploring the characteristics of water, weather, temperature, plants, fish, the built environment, and plumbing systems, I encourage you to follow the children's lead as you present opportunities for learning about the science of water.

The more I learn about water, the more committed I am to protecting it. Sometimes, I also feel overwhelmed by the many concerns and threats to our water resources and our environment. But I've found hope and optimism for the future through my work with children and observing their excitement and curiosity about water science. I hope this book has opened the door to your own sense of hope and excitement as we engage children in learning how to become caring stewards of our planet.

Resources and Recommended Reading

Abell, Tracy. 2017. *How It Works: Toilets.* Focus Readers.

Allen, Pamela. 1996. *Who Sank the Boat?* Puffin Books.

American Chemical Society. 2024. "Heat, Temperature, and Conduction." American Chemical Society. https://www.acs.org/middleschoolchemistry/lessonplans/chapter2/lesson1.html

American Society of Civil Engineers. 2024. "Infrastructure Leaders Building Communities." https://www.asce.org/

Andrews, Elizabeth. 2021. *How Does Plumbing Work?* Cody Koala.

Arbor Day Foundation. 2025. "About Trees: Tree Identification." Arbor Day Foundation. https://www.arborday.org/trees/whattree/

Ashman, Linda. 2020. *When the Storm Comes.* Nancy Paulsen Books.

Asterra. 2022. "Netherlands Dikes and Levees: Effective Flood Defenses." Asterra. https://asterra.io/resources/netherlands-dikes-and-levees/

Bagley, Mary. 2023. "States of Matter: Definition and Phases of Change." LiveScience. https://www.livescience.com/46506-states-of-matter.html

Beatty, Andrea. 2007. *Iggy Peck, Architect.* Abrams Books for Young Readers.

Beckmeyer, Drew. 2023. *I Am a Tornado.* Atheneum Books.

Beran, Crystal. 2023. "How Plants Take Up Water." University of West Virginia Extension. https://extension.wvu.edu/lawn-gardening-pests/lawn-gardening-pests-learning-activities/how-plants-take-up-water

Borenstein, Seth. 2024. "Scientists Find About a Quarter Million Invisible Microplastic Particles in a Liter of Bottled Water." PBS News. https://www.pbs.org/newshour/science/scientists-find-about-a-quarter-million-invisible-microplastic-particles-in-a-liter-of-bottled-water

Boss, Shira. 2023. *The City Tree.* Clarion Books.

Boxer, Elisa. 2022. *One Turtle's Last Straw: The Real-Life Rescue That Sparked a Sea Change.* Crown Books for Young Readers.

Britannica Kids. n.d. "Water Cycle" Britannica Kids. https://kids.britannica.com/kids/article/water-cycle/476333

Britannica Kids. 2025. "Temperature." Britannica Kids. https://kids.britannica.com/students/article/temperature/313807

Brown, Peter. 2009. *The Curious Garden.* Little, Brown.

Burningham, John. 1990. *Mr. Gumpy's Outing.* Square Fish.

Camper, Cathy. 2020. *Ten Ways to Hear Snow.* Kokila.

Carle, Eric. 2005. *10 Little Rubber Ducks.* HarperCollins.

Christakis, Erika. 201 6. *The Importance of Being Little: What Young Children Really Need from Grownups.* Viking.

Cobbs, Vicki. 2003. *I Face the Wind.* HarperCollins.

Constellation. 2025. "What Is Water Conservation?" Constellation. https://www.constellation.com/energy-101/water-conservation-tips0.htm

Denchak, Melissa. 2024. "Flint Water Crisis: Everything You Need to Know." Natural Resources Defense Council. https://www.nrdc.org/stories/flint-water-crisis-everything-you-need-know

Desmond, Jenni. 2015. *The Blue Whale.* Enchanted Lion.

Douglas, Andrew. 2024. "How Many Species of Fish Are There?" World Atlas. https://www.worldatlas.com/animals/how-many-species-of-fish-are-there.html

Duxbury, Alyn C., et al. 2025. "Ocean." Encyclopedia Britannica. https://www.britannica.com/science/ocean

Erikson Institute Early Math Collaborative. 2013. Big Ideas of Early Mathematics: What Teachers of Young Children Need to Know. Pearson.

Fleming, Meg. 2020. *Here Comes Ocean.* Beach Lane Books.

Gadzikowski, Ann. 2020. *Young Architects at Play: STEM Activities for Young Children.* Redleaf Press.

Ghigna, Charles. 2012. *We Need Water.* Picture Window Books.

Gibbons, Gail. 1991. *From Seed to Plant.* Holiday House.

Hassani, Nadia. 2024. "How to Make a Terrarium with Our Easy Step-by-Step Guide." The Spruce. https://www.thespruce.com/how-to-make-terrariums-848007

Hegarty, Stephanie, and Talha Burki. 2024. "Extreme Drought Areas Treble in Size Since 80s—Study." BBC. https://www.bbc.com/news/articles/clyvje458rvo

Helmenstine, Anne. 2021. "Volume Definition in Science." ScienceNotes. https://sciencenotes.org/volume-definition-in-science/

Henkes, Kevin. 2010. *My Garden.* Greenwillow Books.

Hirsh-Pasek, Kathy, et al. 2022. *Where Global Science Meets Playful Learning: Implications for Home, School, Cities and Digital Spaces.* The LEGO Foundation. https://learningthroughplay.com/explore-the-research/where-global-science-meets-playful-learning-implications-for-home-school-cities-and-digital-spaces

Hohn, Donovan. 2012. *Moby-Duck: The True Story of 28,800 Bath Toys Lost at Sea & of the Beachcombers, Oceanographers, Environmentalists & Fools Including the Author Who Went in Search of Them.* Penguin.

Homayoon, Robert. 2024. "How to Make a Paper Boat." WikiHow. https://www.wikihow.com/Make-a-Paper-Boat

Huntington, The. 2025. "Plant Parts." The Huntington. https://www.huntington.org/plant-parts

Hurt, Avery. 2015. "Freshwater Habitat." National Geographic Kids. https://kids.nationalgeographic.com/nature/habitats/article/freshwater

Ingebretsen, Ingrid. n.d. "Toilet to Tap: Drinking Purified Sewage Water." Lifesource Water Systems. https://www.lifesourcewater.com/blog/toilet-to-tap-drinking-purified-sewage-water

Jones Prince, April. 2005. *Twenty-One Elephants and Still Standing.* Clarion Books.

Jordan, Helene J. 2015. *How a Seed Grows.* HarperCollins.

Keats, Ezra Jack. 1962. *The Snowy Day.* Viking Books.

Keegan, Matthew. 2021. "The Rivers That 'Breathe' Greenhouse Gases." BBC. https://www.bbc.com/future/article/20210323-climate-change-the-rivers-that-breathe-greenhouse-gases

Kerley, Barbara. 2002. *A Cool Drink of Water.* National Geographic Kids.

Krasilovsky, Phyllis. 1950. *The Cow Who Fell in the Canal.* Egmont.

Krauss, Ruth. 1945. *The Carrot Seed.* HarperCollins.

Lee, Suzy. 2008. *Wave.* Chronicle Books.

Lindstrom, Carole. 2020. *We Are Water Protectors.* Roaring Brook Press.

Lindstrom, Carole. 2023. *Autumn Peltier, Water Warrior.* Roaring Brook Press.

Lyon, George Ella. 2011. *All the Water in the World.* Atheneum.

Mahroof, Kamran. 2023. "Analysis: How Decorative Glitter Contributes to Microplastic Pollution." PBS News. https://www.pbs.org/newshour/science/analysis-how-decorative-glitter-contributes-to-microplastic-pollution

Majewski, Marc. 2023. *Bridges: A Picture Book.* Harry N. Abrams.

Martin, Jacqueline Briggs. 1999. *Snowflake Bentley.* Houghton Mifflin.

Martin, Marc. 2017. *A River.* Chronicle Books.

McGinty, Alice B. 2021. *The Water Lady: How Darlene Arviso Helps a Thirsty Navajo Nation.* Anne Schwartz Books.

McLeod, Saul. 2024. "Piaget's Preoperational Stage (Ages 2–7)." Simply Psychology. https://www.simplypsychology.org/preoperational.html

McPhail, David. 2022. *I Feel Safe.* Holiday House.

Messner, Kate. 2017. *Over and Under the Pond.* Chronicle Books.

Miyares, Daniel. 2015. *Float.* Simon and Schuster Books for Young Readers.

Moon, Emily Kate. 2021. *Drop: An Adventure through the Water Cycle.* Dial Books.

Mora, Pat. 2020. *Water Rolls, Water Rises.* Lee and Low.

Motum, Markus. 2021. *Ducks Overboard! A True Story of Plastic in Our Oceans.* Walker Books.

National Aeronautics and Space Administration. 2021. "Phases of Matter." NASA. https://www.grc.nasa.gov/www/k-12/rocket/state.html

National Association for the Education of Young Children. n.d. "Interested in Accreditation?" NAEYC. https://www.naeyc.org/accreditation/early-learning/interested

National Association for the Education of Young Children. 2022. *NAEYC Early Learning Program Accreditation Standards and Assessment Items.* NAEYC.

Nature Conservancy, The. n.d. "Charting a Future for the Colorado River." The Nature Conservancy. https://www.nature.org/en-us/about-us/where-we-work/united-states/colorado/stories-in-colorado/colorado-charting-a-future-for-colorado-river/

National Geographic Society. 2012. "Fish Pictures and Facts." National Geographic. https://www.nationalgeographic.com/animals/fish

National Geographic Society. 2023. "Sea Level Rise." National Geographic Education. https://education.nationalgeographic.org/resource/sea-level-rise/

National Geographic Society. 2024. "Dams." National Geographic Education. https://education.nationalgeographic.org/resource/dams/

National Geographic Society. 2025. "Photosynthesis." National Geographic Education. https://education.nationalgeographic.org/resource/photosynthesis/

National Oceanic and Atmospheric Administration. 2023. "The Hydrologic Cycle." NOAA. https://www.noaa.gov/jetstream/atmosphere/hydro

National Oceanic and Atmospheric Administration. 2025. "Careers in Hydrology." NOAA. https://www.noaa.gov/careers/hydrology

National Research Council. 2016. "Kindergarten Topics Model." Next Generation Science Standards. https://www.nextgenscience.org/kindergarten-topics-model

National Science Teachers Association. 2014. "NSTA Position Statement: Early Childhood Science Education." Position statement. NSTA. https://www.nsta.org/nstas-official-positions/early-childhood-science-education

Nelson, Robin. 2003. *Freezing and Melting*. Lerner Classroom.

Onion, Amanda. 2023. "Why Is the Ocean Different Colors in Different Places?" HowStuffWorks. https://science.howstuffworks.com/environmental/earth/oceanography/why-is-ocean-different-colors-different-places.htm

Paul, Miranda. 2015. *Water Is Water.* Roaring Brook Press.

Petruzzello, Melissa. 2022. "Why Is There Fresh and Salt Water on Earth?" Encyclopedia Britannica. https://www.britannica.com/story/why-is-there-fresh-and-salt-water-on-earth

Portis, Antoinette. 2019. *Hey, Water!* Neal Porter Books.

Rey, H.A. 2010. *Curious George, Plumber's Helper*. Clarion Books.

Rockwell, Anne. 2008. *Clouds*. HarperCollins.

Rosenstock, Barb. 2024. *Great Lakes: Our Freshwater Treasure*. Knopf.

Sakkas, Chrisos, and Stavroula Samartzi. 2024. "5-Year-Old Children Performing Piaget's Liquid Conservation Tasks Demonstrated in Physical and Digital Environment." *International Journal of Psychological Studies* 16(1): 61–69. doi:10.5539/ijps.v16n1p61

Sayre, April Pulley. 2016. *Best in Snow*. Beach Lane Books.

Shaw, Gina. 2016. *Curious About Snow*. Grosset & Dunlap.

Shumaker, Debra Kempf. 2021. *Freaky, Funky Fish: Odd Facts About Fascinating Fish*. Running Press Kids.

Srinivasan, Divya. 2020. *Little Owl's Snow*. Viking.

Stewart, Ken. 2023. "Buoyancy." Encyclopedia Britannica. https://www.britannica.com/science/buoyancy

Tan, Zhai Yun. 2016. "How Do We Get Our Drinking Water in the U.S.?" NPR. https://www.npr.org/2016/04/14/473806134/how-do-we-get-our-drinking-water-in-the-u-s

United Nations. n.d. "We Must Act Now to Avert Global Water Crisis." United Nations Global Compact. https://unglobalcompact.org/take-action/20th-anniversary-campaign/we-must-act-now-to-avert-global-water-crisis

UCLA Health. 2022. "15 Foods That Help You Stay Hydrated." UCLA Health. https://www.uclahealth.org/news/article/15-food-that-help-you-stay-hydrated

U.S. Department of Agriculture. n.d. "Extreme Weather." U.S. Department of Agriculture. https://www.climatehubs.usda.gov/content/extreme-weather

U.S. Department of Health and Human Services, Administration for Children and Families, Office of Head Start. n.d. "Interactive Head Start Early Learning Outcomes Framework: Ages Birth to Five." Head Start.gov. https://eclkc.ohs.acf.hhs.gov/interactive-head-start-early-learning-outcomes-framework-ages-birth-five

U.S. Department of Health and Human Services, Administration for Children and Families, Office of Head Start. 2015. *Head Start Early Learning Outcomes Framework: Ages Birth to Five*. https://www.govinfo.gov/content/pkg/GOVPUB-HE23_1100-PURLgpo65456/pdf/GOVPUB-HE23_1100-PURL-gpo65456.pdf

U.S. Geological Survey. 2018a. "Irrigation Water Use." Water Science School. https://www.usgs.gov/special-topics/water-science-school/science/irrigation-water-use#overview

U.S. Geological Survey. 2018b. "Water Color." Water Science School. https://www.usgs.gov/special-topics/water-science-school/science/water-color

U.S. Geological Survey. 2024. "How Much Natural Water Is There?" USGS. https://www.usgs.gov/faqs/how-much-natural-water-there Verde, Susan. 2016. *The Water Princess*. G. P. Putnam and Sons.

Vespa, Emily. 2024. "Post-Helene, Mental Health Providers Help Kids Cope." NC Health News. https://www.northcarolinahealthnews.org/2024/10/18/post-helene-mental-health-providers-help-kids-cope/

Whitmore-Williams, Susan C., Christie Manning, Kirra Krygsman, and Meighen Speiser. 2017. *Mental Health and Our Changing Climate: Impacts, Implications and Guidance. American Psychological Association*. https://www.apa.org/news/press/releases/2017/03/mental-health-climate.pdf

Willems, Mo. 2011. *Should I Share My Ice Cream?* Hyperion.

Wilsdon, Christina. 2016. *Ultimate Oceanpedia*. National Geographic Kids.

Worthington, Niles. 2015. *A Plumber's Job*. Cavendish Square.

Zosh, Jennifer M., et al. 2017. *Learning through Play: A Review of the Evidence*. White paper. The LEGO Foundation.

Zumdahl, Steven S. 2025. "Water." Encyclopedia Britannica. https://www.britannica.com/science/water

Index